MY THOUGHTS, MY FEELINGS

Edited By Byron Tobolik

First published in Great Britain in 2023 by:

Young Writers
Remus House
Coltsfoot Drive
Peterborough
PE2 9BF
Telephone: 01733 890066
Website: www.youngwriters.co.uk

All Rights Reserved
Book Design by Ashley Janson
© Copyright Contributors 2023
Softback ISBN 978-1-83565-023-3

Printed and bound in the UK by BookPrintingUK
Website: www.bookprintinguk.com
YB0572R

FOREWORD

For Young Writers' latest competition This Is Me, we asked primary school pupils to look inside themselves, to think about what makes them unique, and then write a poem about it! They rose to the challenge magnificently and the result is this fantastic collection of poems in a variety of poetic styles.

Here at Young Writers our aim is to encourage creativity in children and to inspire a love of the written word, so it's great to get such an amazing response, with some absolutely fantastic poems. It's important for children to focus on and celebrate themselves and this competition allowed them to write freely and honestly, celebrating what makes them great, expressing their hopes and fears, or simply writing about their favourite things. This Is Me gave them the power of words. The result is a collection of inspirational and moving poems that also showcase their creativity and writing ability.

I'd like to congratulate all the young poets in this anthology, I hope this inspires them to continue with their creative writing.

CONTENTS

Independent Entrants

Hannah Jiang (9)	1
Amber XinTi Wang (10)	2
Pippa Oakes (10)	6
Saumya Kulkarni (10)	9
Mali Charles (8)	10
Ayman Taslim	12
Farida Abdulgawad (11)	14
Thomas Maddison (7)	16
Genesis Brown (11)	18
Esmé Meehan (7)	21
Janna Oyedeji (10)	22
Ella Ingram (11)	24
Jack Morgan (8)	26
Elektra O'Riordan (8)	28
Hibah Ahmad (7)	31
Mehreen Azim	32
Saanvika Anemoni (10)	34
Carmella Ha (10)	36
Emmanuel Olofinlade (8)	38
Daisy Nowak (9)	40
Aarav Veer Singh Baxi (11)	42
Abheer Shetty (10)	44
Eleanor Pringle (8)	46
Ned English (11)	48
Daisy Rendle (11)	50
Sam Lee (8)	52
Himavarsha Manchikanti (10)	54
Eddie Chen (9)	56
Mariana Abreu Fernandes (11)	58
Chloë Grindal (11)	60
Athena Christopher (10)	62
Grace Jarrett (11)	64
Oluwanifemi Adejobi (8)	66
Javen Matthew Colaco (10)	68
Amelia Frappell (9)	70
Finley Churchill (8)	72
Jet-Leigh O'Riordan (10)	74
Maxim Johansson (8)	76
Hudson Lang (8)	78
Esther Mbogol (10)	80
Ruby Kingston (9)	82
Amelia Poon (8)	84
Shaily Mudholkar (7)	86
Mohammed Adil Ahmad (10)	88
Charlotte Easter (11)	90
Jasmine Koc (10)	92
Zoe Smaldon (11)	94
Khadijah Miller-Nash (9)	95
Sefa Samuel Adura (9)	96
Stanley Brewster (9)	97
Pia Pradhan (11)	98
Yusuf Rana (9)	100
Robin Davies (8)	102
Atlas Devrimoz (9)	104
Clinton Newman (8)	105
Aminah Badjan (11)	106
Vesta Ulozaite (9)	107
Niniola-Gabriel Abayomi (7)	108
Lucian Moore (6)	110
Farah Karim (10)	112
Eshan Pal (9)	113
Jessica Thorne (9)	114
Alyssa-Grace Harriette (11)	116
Starlar Ho (8)	117
Shaylan Somal (10)	118
Esmae Emin-Wyatt (10)	119
Liberty Bridges (10)	120
Nyla Kabir (7)	122
Maariya Bhamji (10)	124

Name	Page	Name	Page
Faye Convery (9)	125	Charlotte Sugden (8)	174
William Thompson (9)	126	Imogen Cobley (11)	175
Kangti Li (10)	127	Aarav Dhiman (9)	176
Sky Kwok (9)	128	Summayyah Hoque (8)	177
Rita Krasnici (9)	130	Orla Hamilton (10)	178
Shreeya Arora (8)	132	Evan Senanayake (10)	179
Oujj Shah (11)	134	Gurmeen Kaur (11)	180
Hector Gathorne-Hardy (9)	135	Nevaeh Pancholi (7)	181
Shravya Shrivastava (10)	136	Zoya Iqbal	182
Lily Ingrey-Counter (11)	138	Jeremiah Amoah (7)	183
Connie Farley-Hills (7)	139	Sargam Shrotri (7)	184
Mishka Saxena (7)	140	Jake Brzezinski (6)	185
Lilly Rai Hardey (6)	141	Roberta Huhn (11)	186
Melina-Rose Papalambrou (9)	142	James Bass (10)	187
Lucy Davies	144	Erick Karim (8)	188
Harvey John Morton (9)	145	Victoria-Dorinda Ametefe (10)	189
Sebastian Mihai (10)	146	Zahra Mukhtar Zia (10)	190
Josiah Amoah (7)	147	Sarwan Bains (8)	191
Raeesah Khan (10)	148	Charlotte Holmes (9)	192
Joshua Ahmed (10)	149	Cristina Alvanos (10)	193
Maria Miah (11)	150	Corey James Clark (9)	194
Muhammed Zeshan Aariz Wehvaria (8)	151	Malaika Gumbo (9)	195
		Paige Graham (10)	196
Jeeva Jandu (8)	152	Jacob Payne (10)	197
Michelle Akadiri (9)	153	Lucas Varney (9)	198
Charley Biereth-Purcell	154	Svitlana Rakul (8)	199
Daisy Campbell (9)	155	Evisa Dragoba (9)	200
Sacha Kasmi (11)	156	Sonya Scott (10)	201
Hannah Roper (10)	158	Bradyn Pancholi (9)	202
Isobel Sloan (7)	160	Florence McDaid (9)	203
Alice Walton (9)	161	Liv (11)	204
Brandon Tailor-Hooker (11)	162	Somer Howell (8)	205
Nikolas Kornelakis (8)	163	Isabelle Djumpah-Ansah (10)	206
Grace Ash (12)	164	Lily McKeon (10)	207
Skye Tallowin (8)	165	Kaisea-Rose Brayshaw (11)	208
Manha Abdullah (10)	166	Ben Allison (11)	209
Khadija Aktar (11)	167	Hamzah Rahman (10)	210
Ryan Haque (9)	168	Akshayan Vivekanantharajah	211
Sarah Tossou Gbete (10)	169	Syeda Anisa Mumtaz Nakvi (10)	212
Alia McWilliams (10)	170	Lauren Bennett Lazare (10)	213
Hartley Taylor-Richardson (8)	171	Sienna Somal (8)	214
Issabelle Ord (9)	172	Isabella Howes-Warnes (10)	215
Shahnoor Zahra Khan (5)	173	Rose Le Mer Suresh (7)	216

Name	Page
Aminah Zishan (8)	217
Syeda Anisa Mumtaz Nakvi (10)	218
Noah Tailor-Hooker (11)	219
Ethan Jones (8)	220
Samuel Kiwanuka-Musoke (7)	221
Neha Shivapathy (7)	222
Ranniel Masambique (11)	223
Princess Chelsea Ogbogu-Asogwa (10)	224
Levi Amoah (8)	225
Jake Perry (9)	226
Delia Barnham (10)	227
Alexander Thomas Elmantawy (8)	228
Sophie Pegler (8)	229
Maame Gyamfuah Boateng-Bamdoh (9)	230
Cosmas Eze (11)	231
Harrison Pronger (8)	232
Markel Marinho (10)	233
Saviour Higgans (8)	234
Oscar Cormack (8)	235
Jack Sadler (11)	236
Amy Smiley (15)	237
Sophia Junglas (8)	238
Andreea Maria Alexe (8)	239
Olivia Chidwick (11)	240
Harry Warren (9)	241
Thomas Potter (11)	242
William Hogley (11)	243
Sophie Goodier (11)	244
Nancy Rossiter-Pointer (10)	245
Conrad Jones (8)	246
Charlie Thomas (8)	247
Zuriel Oyedeji (8)	248
Blake Lagoda (10)	249
Xander Blyth Bell (9)	250
Amelia Reilly (10)	251
Victor Umahi Ndiwe (11)	252
Sienna Jefferson (8)	253
Archie Pugh (7)	254
Tanya Huhn (11)	255
Harry Chalk (9)	256
Chloe Rose (8)	257
Muhammed Luqman Arafath (7)	258
Elizabeth Dymond (9)	259
Charlotte Bundred (10)	260
Julia Falecka (11)	261
Safa Khalil	262
Rabia Dar (11)	263
Rose Blundell (10)	264

THE POEMS

Butterfly And I

Every butterfly starts as a caterpillar, munching on verdant leaves, like this one:
Playing with her wriggly friends, under her parents' watchful wings,
Wandering the cold misty floors of the only home she knows.
As she frolics in the giant green gardens of England,
Finding more interesting creatures to befriend,
She awaits eagerly what she will be,
Too soon it's time to hibernate,
Bundled in a silky cocoon
So she is changing daily now,
And emerges, waking from slumber,
To find new sights, new smells, new views,
Waiting for her as she adjusts to her new high-rise home,
And as she unfurls her gossamer wings, in the hot humid air,
It is time for the fresh-formed butterfly to take to the sky for the first time...
She flaps her wings - and flies - and I realise it's time for me to thrive in Hong Kong.

Hannah Jiang (9)

Maze Of My Mind

Defiant muse of words
Do sing
To such a voyager in the starry night
Whose feet ache from the assaults of rock and balm
Whose head grows heavy with memories take
And whose hands tremble to navigate

Deep inside
I know where the stars will guide
This burning flame of melody
In the labyrinth of my mind -
Who knows where that may be?

Over the glassy, turquoise seas
Over the mountaintops of spiralling chalk
Far over the fields of earthly green
Through the dark blemishes of night
That fold, twine
The blushes of the moon
Dark, dark, pitch of darkness fold
Melody be

Melody gone
Drowned in this music of life

And when the rays of golden dawn
Take night's reign out and out and out
Here in the misty lands
Of budding bronze leaves
Will I wait
For that sunshine
To never abate

Here in the misty lands
Where I live deep
We tell honeysuckle stories
Of not one single crochet beat
But a multitude of fluting tones
And here the stories flood
And grow vibrant
And find their golden blood

That tremulous ichor that dribbles out of the sky
Doth make my musings
Half of the sprightly surprise
When in the mornings the birds do tweet

I pause and ponder
That glorious well I live in deep

And here I will stay
Basking in the ichor of words
Waiting for the sunshine to reach
Reach
Reach
Reach out, with silver hands
And take the night
And take the dawn of dun
And bring in the cresting of the sun

Here my feet ache again
But less of a burden
Less of the strain
That labyrinth of my mind
Doth take and give in kind

For here in the misty lands
We imagine
An eye closed to set tangents off
The trickling toffee of the morning
A zillion beats of hot and cold

Always, always, to be bold
And everlasting, not to be told
That time ticking steadily on
Like Alice's rabbit of a furlong
Yet steadily our hourglasses drained
Yet clipped our manuscripts wane
Yet magic in our leaves
Yet paler our ease

Over the spider-glass cliffs
Over the crackly rain of turf
Feet do ache
Feet do pause
Labyrinth that leads me on

Defiant muse of words do sing
To me of that traveller in the misty lands old
And once a wanderer
And once a stranger
Now's the time to be bold
And here my tale cuts to an end
So this story - all but told.

Amber XinTi Wang (10)

The Doom And No Gloom

This world is full of doom,
Look around and see the flowers so gloom,
No more beautiful blossoms bloom,
Oh this world is so doomed.

Here comes the sun beaming down,
All the doom be fleeing now,
The daisies bloom and the butterflies play,
All the happiness comes today,
Oh what a beautiful sound,
The bees buzz as they fly around.
Oh what a beautiful day.

Woke up this morning by the bees' play,
Seems like happiness arrived today,
No more sorrow and no more doom,
Look around, oh such beautiful blossoms bloom.

Wake up again, no fun being had,
No buzzing bees, wonder why everyone is so sad?
No laughter, no play,
No nothing at all, no fun being had.

What's wrong with this world?
We slash and we burn, we abuse and we torture,
We mistreat the world, put it through so much exhaustion,
We need to put an end to this living torture.

This living torture is what we created,
What did the world do to be hated?
All it does is provide for us with life
As we are taking the world away, that's not very nice!

Take a look around and see the beauty that could be,
The only colour the naked eye can see is probably that dying bee.
What is our future generations going to think of all this racket and hate,
When all this work did was create?

Pollution, pollution is all in the air,
This is not just affecting humans, it is even affecting polar bears
And that is not fair,

The ice is collapsing, the skies are getting warmer and warmer,
One day we are going to wake up and realise
The world is hurting from all the trauma.

Pippa Oakes (10)

This Is Me

This is me trying to be as clever as can be
I'm a bit clumsy, aside from that I'm hilarious and funny
I love unicorns and rainbows, and the sky and space interest me a lot
I'm as kind as a puppy and as calm as a cat and, of course, I like to wear hats
I like to listen to music whenever I can, and when I can, I'm happy and glad
I'll help someone whenever they need it, no matter the reason
I try to be as generous as I can and if I am, people are glad
I love drawing very much, I have lots of good luck
My favourite colours are pink, purple and blue, and blue is the sky's hue
For me, reading is a pleasure that should not be measured
My favourite animal is a Pegasus, and they can fly whatever day it is
Overall, that was me and if you enjoyed reading this, it'll fill me with glee.

Saumya Kulkarni (10)

This Is Me

In Wales, there dwells a girl named Mali Bright,
With ginger hair that burns like sunset's light.
An eight-year-old, so full of life and glee,
This is Mali, this is me, and I am free.

Two dads, Dadi and Dada, by her side,
Their love and care, in them, she does confide.
With little Osian, just a toddler, too,
Their family's love, a bond forever true.

Passion for the Earth, for nature's grace,
Sustainability, her guiding embrace.
Her local park, a haven to explore,
Where dreams take flight, and Mali does implore.

To sing, create, and make the world her own,
A future scientist, seeds of knowledge sown.
An engineer, perhaps, with vision vast,
In Mali's dreams, the future is steadfast.

A vegan heart, compassion for all creatures,
A soul that treasures life's myriad features.
She loves to swim, to act, to take the stage,
In drama's arms, she finds her heartfelt page.

Brownies and piano, skills she's honing,
A spirit bright and ever so enthralling.
Role models many, she aspires to be,
From Katniss to Greta, her heart runs free.

Michelle, Amelia, Buffy, strong and bold,
Billie, Taylor, their stories she's told.
A feminist's heart beats within her chest,
For equal rights, she stands with all the rest.

She fights for justice, let the banners unfurl,
For people of all races, boys and girls.
Love knows no bounds, in Mali's heart, it swells,
Equality for all, the story she tells.

In Mali's world, where dreams and hopes align,
A soul so pure, a spirit so divine.
This is Mali, a beacon in the night,
With love and passion, she'll set the world alight.

Mali Charles (8)

This Is Me

I am what I am; it's down to me
Forging a path along the way
With plenty to do and lots to say.
Things to do and lots to see.
Eager to try and ready to be
I am what I am; it's down to me.

Maths, science, English too,
Subjects I really like to do
Whatever the weather, come rain or shine
Playing football with my friends is divine.
That is what I aim to be
I am what I am; it's down to me.

Once at home, I like to unwind,
Computer games are on my mind
Taking me away to another world
Where senses and pleasures are unfurled.
This is when I begin to feel free
I am what I am; it's down to me.

At night in bed, I like to read
My mind is open and doesn't impede
The thrill of turning a fresh new page
With wonders appearing for any age.
Spiders and darkness do stay with me
I am what I am; that's me you see.

Aiding others is a balm to my soul
To see them flourish is my own true goal
A gesture here and a kindness there
Makes me happy, it's in the air.
Helping people comes naturally
I am what I am; it's up to me.

The world is a mass of wondrous tones
Sights unseen and sounds unknown,
Injustice lurks, with things I can't change
Upsets my being all the same,
But Mother's chicken and my new cat
Coming to sit on my nice warm lap.
All this makes me look forward to see
I am what I am; and this is me.

Ayman Taslim

Breast Cancer Awareness!

In the month of pink, let's raise our voice,
To spread awareness, make a choice.

Breast cancer, a battle we must fight,
Together, we'll shine, like a star at night.

A disease that strikes, with a cunning hand,
Affects women and men, across the land.

Early detection, the key to survive,
Let us unite and keep hope alive.

Ladies, be aware, examine and feel,
Your breasts, your protector, are a big deal.

A simple self-check might seem small,
But it could save your life and save us all.

Doctors and nurses, they hold the key,
Screening tests, a guide you'll be.

Encourage the women, every race, every age,
To detect any changes, turn the page.

Support groups gather, with love to embrace,
Survivors and fighters, share their grace.

Their courage inspires, a beacon so bright,
We stand by their side, with all our might.

Radiation and chemo, surgeries endured,
Sacrifice made; strength assured.

But in their eyes, a spirit that's strong,
Defying odds, singing a victory song.

Let's educate, empower our nation,
Spread the word and create a sensation.

Fund research, find a cure we seek,
Erasing the plague, finally, we'll break.

So come wear pink, let's make a stand,
Hand in hand together we expand.

The message of hope, the call to empower,
Breast cancer awareness, every minute, every hour.

Farida Abdulgawad (11)

Snap, Crackle, Pop

My classroom is a forest floor
And every time I flap,
A twig catches under my shoe
Snap, snap, snap.
Do this, do that, do as I say
Snap, snap, snap.
It hurts, I want to run away
Snap, snap, snap.

My feet are moving fast, I feel alive and free, *but*
Crackle, crackle, crackle, sound of the twigs under my feet.

They tell me to *slow, stop, breathe,*
But all that I can think
is the overwhelming *crackle*
of my focus on the brink.

My body isn't doing what I'm asking it to do,
Crackle, crackle, crackle, as more energy
flows through.

This Is Me - My Thoughts, My Feelings

Try to connect, hold on,
It only shivers away
to communicate I laugh, but
Pop, I cannot move my way.

I cannot control myself,
Malfunctioning electric,
I'm wrong as I hurt others.
I didn't want to do it.
Striking out and scared,
Pop.
Lonely and unheard,
Pop.
I scream and scream and scream and scream,
Pop, pop, POP.

After the earthquake settles down, I'm floating in deep space,
Reaching out to reconnect in a constant,
caring place.
I never was abandoned, I hear them gently say,
as back into the classroom we hug, hum and sway.
Snap, crackle, POP!

Thomas Maddison (7)

All About Me

This is my life
You arrived just in time
I'm in with the rhymes
I love to draw
Praw, braw, draw
Same with singing
Now I'm singing
I love my mum so much
Stew chicken is my favourite
My favourite, my favourite, my favourite
I was at the GO-FEST stage
In a jumping way
Me and my friends did a performance
I was doing my own solo
We also had a school photo
I was beatboxing and playing the ukulele
Bukulee, wukeulee, dakuleele
We were dancing and singing
With the joy that we were bringing
I was doing saxophone playing
With no delaying

Getting into the groove
With things to improve
Needing some practice
Like an actress
Doing new songs
Pong, dong, bong
Hearing them every Saturday
Similar to a music gallery
My favourite thing to draw is Sonic
That rhymes with comic
He is super-fast
When going to blast
With his abilities
The speedy activities
I watched that movie in the summer
I was making recycled things
Bings, ping, dings
Starting with a cardboard box
That is shaped like blocks
Using parts of bottles
Cooking like a model

Which were big eyes
I have never seen that in my life
Having a nice slide
With a very cool creative ride.

Genesis Brown (11)

This Is Me, Amazing Esmé

This is me, Esmé!
I'm crazy and energetic, running here and there
With my sparkling blue eyes and my wild, red hair.

This is me! I like gymnastics,
I'm like an adventurous spider monkey,
Leaping through the canopy, jumping, swinging, so much fun feeling so free!

This is me! I like nature and animals
I'm a daredevil climber, fearless and playful like a bear,
When I grow up, I want to be an animal rescuer for all the animals that need my care.

This is me! I like dancing
What I like best are dancing and prancing to my favourite beat,
Twirling and spinning, always moving my feet

This is me! I like playing music
My fingers are speedy, as quick as a flash with my rockin' keyboard and my noisy flute,
All of these things are never on mute.

Esmé Meehan (7)

It's A Pleasure To Be Me!

I'm a ten-year-old girl full of zest,
In October, Black History is the best!
It's my pleasure to share a bit about me,
I'm part of the future and history, you see.

I adore books, some say I'm quite a nerd,
But reading's my pleasure, and that's only my word!
Books open doors, shaping our actions,
In literary worlds, I find my attractions.

Math, it's a mix of simple and complex,
Sometimes I feel like I'm caught in a vortex.
I tackle each problem, one by one,
To finally raise my hand, proudly saying, "I'm done!"

Art can be tricky, that's very true,
But I believe in 'yet', that's what I'll do.
Sometimes I surprise myself, even though I'm not a pro,
When my art's displayed, it makes me glow.

I have asthma, but it doesn't define me,
In sports like football, I'm lively and free.
Tournaments are where I shine, you see,
Like a bright ornament, full of glee.

I'm a ten-year-old girl full of zest, it's true!
In October, I celebrate Black History with you.
I hope you've enjoyed learning a bit about me,
I'm a piece of the future and our shared history.

Janna Oyedeji (10)

My Life

English, science, Spanish, French,
There's a thirst I cannot quench.
This thirst, as I say, is a thirst for facts,
And to be satisfied I have to get it exact.

This horrible standard follows like a plague,
And I feel so frustrated when an answer is vague.
Answer me, please! And please be specific,
The answers I seek are deeper than the Pacific.

My humour cannot always be understood,
Which makes me feel I talk more than I should.
My kindness, which can prove to be extensive,
Is not rewarded as such, as acknowledgement is expensive.

My life, like all others, is oddly jumbled,
But the tragedies I face leave me strangely humbled.
But such is the price of living a life,
You can't get a good one without any strife.

My books and my music are quite different from others,
They inspire me to write about families and lovers,
Or death and destruction, it depends on my mood,
Or if I am lazy, my stories are quite crude.

That is my life, I hope you didn't find it too boring,
My ambitions are many, my hopes now are soaring.
I hope you found it an interesting read,
I hope you were listening, I hope you paid heed.

Ella Ingram (11)

This Is Me

Loud: noises and sounds
Word: words of interest to talk and speak
Play: bounce and run around
Act: mime, scream and shout
TV, pad, TV, pad, TV, pad, TV, pad
Share: who cares? It will come
Dirt, mess, touch and feel
Stretch, turn and roll around
Throw, drop and catch
Listen, watch and learn
Push, pull and twist
Hide, tuck and sleep
Mud, water, sea and sand
Stretch, twist and turn
Taste, eat, hate and enjoy
Sun, rain, wind and snow
Tall, loud and proud
Laugh, joke and fool around
Smile, cry and 'angry monkey'
Quiet: shush to be shushed
Alone: dark and unaware

Joy: happiness in a world of my own
Moment: episode, maybe a meltdown
Learn: take in and be taught
Sponge: develop and grow
Danger: don't, it will hurt you
Swing: park - "Push, please!"
Grass, plants, soil and grow
Gruffalo, Zog, Hey Duggee, Teletubbies,
In the Night Garden and The Croods
Jurassic, Kong, movies and songs
Animals, zoos, farms,
Swimming and daffodils
Fear: unknown, what's next?
Love: lovable and loved
Independence: we just don't know
This is me, just Jack with ASD.

Jack Morgan (8)

This Is Me!

This is me!
Elektra with an E
There are so many things that I want to be
Now that I am no longer three.

This is me!
I can sing like the birds in the trees
In any key
From A and B to C and D

This is me!
I like carrots and pink
7Up is my favourite drink
I can do what I think
Fall asleep in a blink

This is me!
I like honey and cheese
The birds and the bees
Making ice pops when they freeze
I say thank you and please

This is me!
I play with my tea set
And pretend to drink tea
I pour the milk quite beautifully
And then drink it carefully

This is me!
I play with my friends all day
We can make the rain go away
We can make the sunshine stay
When we have a great day

This is me!
I'm happy when I scream
I like eating ice cream
I have nightmares when I dream
My mom and I make a great team

This is me!
I am not a liar
When I swing, I can get higher and higher
I don't like to play with fire

I can play all day and I never ever tire
When I was a baby
I was quite the crier!

Elektra O'Riordan (8)

This Is Me

Hibah is my name
I am a seven-year-old girl,
I love to dress up and do twirls.

Islam is my religion,
my favourite bird is a pigeon,
I love using my imagination,
I adore all of God's creations.

Being inventive is my passion,
I have a deep affection with fashion,
I enjoy learning and love to sing,
Going to school is my favourite thing.

Achievements of mine are winning an art competition,
Doing incredibly well in life is my mission.

Helping my mum and my family makes me feel happy,
Sometimes I try to change my sister's nappy.
Hobbies of mine are reading and drawing,
I like to eat chicken nuggets they taste so divine.

Hibah Ahmad (7)

Betrayal

You said you loved me, you said you cared,
But then you left me, alone and scared.
You broke my heart, you tore it apart,
You betrayed me, right from the start.

Betrayal, betrayal, how could you do this to me?
Betrayal, betrayal, you were the one I trusted.
Betrayal, betrayal, now I'm left in misery,
Betrayal, betrayal, our friendship is now dusted.

You lied to me, you cheated with me,
You played with me like I was a toy.
You made me cry.

Betrayal, betrayal, how could you do this to me?
Betrayal, betrayal, you were the one I trusted.
Betrayal, betrayal, now I'm left in misery,
Betrayal, betrayal, our friendship is now dusted.

Now I'm alone, in this cold world,
Trying to heal from this pain you caused.
But I can't forget what you did to me,
You betrayed me, and that's unforgivable.

Betrayal, betrayal, how could you do this to me?
Betrayal, betrayal, you were the one I trusted.
Betrayal, betrayal, now I'm left in misery,
Betrayal, betrayal, our friendship is now dusted.

You made me sigh,
You betrayed me without saying goodbye.

Betrayal, betrayal...

Mehreen Azim

Me

I'm a 10-year-old girl full of life's delight,
With a heart that's pure like a starry night.
In my world of dreams, I take my stand,
A world of wonder in my little hand.

I love hamsters with their furry grace,
Their tiny paws and their tiny space.
In my room, they find their joyful play,
Running, exploring, each and every day.

With a hamster wheel and mazes to explore,
Their antics leave me wanting more and more.
I watch them closely, their every move,
In their world of wonder, I truly groove.

But there's more to me beyond this theme,
I'm a young soul with a sparkling gleam.
Learning and growing, day by day,
In this journey of life, I find my way.

With dreams and hopes that soar so high,
In this world, I'll reach for the sky.
A 10-year-old girl with a heart so true,
With endless possibilities to pursue.

So, remember me, as I continue to grow,
In this adventure of life, watch me glow.
A 10-year-old girl with dreams untamed,
In my heart, the world is forever framed.

Saanvika Anemoni (10)

My Primary Life

My life is an experience
Each year I grew
But each time that happened,
I learnt something new

I'll start in reception,
Oh, that was divine
Finger-painting all day
Not something I could decline

Next in Year One
We went to London Zoo
Wrote words and read books
Something I could pursue

Year Two was next
That's when Covid started,
Lockdown and viruses
My class was parted

Year Three - that was fun
Egyptians and the Romans
Moving up to Key Stage Two
Alas, a history devotion

Year Four, a big adventure,
Making new friends along the way,
Learning upstairs, that was new
A fun year, I'd say

Year Five, I had it in the bag
Probably my best year yet
English, Maths, DT and history
A year I'll never forget

Year Six, here at last
PGL and SATs
Lots to come this year
Succeed primary, perhaps?

That's all my life so far
I enjoyed it a lot
But I keep writing,
I'll remember the memories I forgot.

Carmella Ha (10)

This Is Me

My skin is chocolate brown,
And you'll never have a frown,
When I'm there, hanging around.
My school uniform is violet,
And my face is smile-lit.
I am joyful.
You'll see me running at the speed of sound
With chains broken, I have no worries taking me down
I've said it before and will say it again:
I am strong and will use the smartness I've gained.
I am smart.
Sometimes at school, I feel like I'm different from the others
Because they're acting like sisters and brothers.
But I still remember my little phrase:
'People are never the same'!
So, I walk into my class,
All proud and brave,
'Cause now I know that people aren't the same
I will talk and say this like a speech

To tell you this now, so listen to me teach:
If you feel different from everyone else
Just be brave and act like yourself
So now you know all about me
And the techniques I've used to see
You also know I am me
And no one can take that away from me!

Emmanuel Olofinlade (8)

Take A Breath

Screams and crushes everywhere, in your head and in the air
When you know something isn't right, don't take a chocolate and take a bite
Instead,
Take a breath, take a breath, take a breath...
Working hard like a busy bee, go on holiday, can't you see?
When you feel stressed, think of all - you are blessed!
Don't worry or feel sorry
Instead, take a breath!
Go on, smile even if your work is a massive pile
I know, it's hard especially when you are scared.
Come on in and join our party!
If you don't know how then I will tell you now
Just, take a breath...
I know, I know, you want to be popular, even if it's just a blur
You should know that you're unique
Who knows, you might soon have your own boutique!

When you reach for a star, I promise you, you will go far
Also, be kind and helpful too, then you won't lose your shoe.
This time for fun, so you can be as bright as the sun,
Take a breath, take a breath, take a breath!

Daisy Nowak (9)

The Kitchen When I Was A Boy

Ketchup stains on the walls,
Orange juice spilt on the floors,
In the kitchen when I was a boy.
My brother Zach with all his toys,
Being thrown around and in the drawers,
In the kitchen when I was a boy.
Fried eggs and sizzling bacon,
The smells I remember when I had awakened,
In the kitchen when I was a boy.
The rack of knives up on the shelves,
That we weren't allowed to touch ourselves,
In the kitchen when I was a boy.
Greasy plates and half-finished drinks,
Beginning to pile up in the sink,
In the kitchen when I was a boy.
One Christmas, I remember it well,
Mum made Christmas pudding, oh what a smell!
Dad made turkey, so juicy and plump,
But after dinner, he was so full, he slumped!

In the kitchen when I was a boy.
These are the memories I had as a boy,
From Christmas dinner to playing with toys,
I had fun when I was a kid,
And I will never forget the things that I did,
In the kitchen when I was a boy.

Aarav Veer Singh Baxi (11)

This Is Me

Ambition
My dream is to become a star cricketer
And make my parents proud of me

Empathy
When I see someone without eyes
I feel their pain and I wish
I could bring a smile on their face

I Like Myself
I know how to adjust, understand situations
Rather than asking too many questions

I Admire... You
She is the one who sees me grow every day
Who pampers me and loves me unconditionally
No comparison to her never-ending love
Can you guess who she is
Her title is famous in Egypt
Guess?
Her title has five letters...

What Makes Me Happy
If I forget the things which made me sad
I will be happy

Dream
I'd love to represent my country
As one of the best cricket batsmen

Personification
My giggle makes flowers bloom again

What Makes Me?
I am a kind, charming, loving
And happy fun-filled little boy.

Abheer Shetty (10)

Love Always Wins

"Love always wins," my mom told me one night,
"When hate rises to the top, love puts up a fight."
"But when will hate stop?" I asked her again.
"Ah, patience, my love, it only began!"
"I know you want Dad, and I want him too!
But we'll have to wait a year or a few."
"How long will the war be?"
"Quite long, my dear, hate won't stop until love disappears!"
"Will it disappear? Love, I mean."
"Never! And when things get tough, love intervenes!"
"I miss Dad," I said solemnly.
"I know, but he's out digging trenches, probably."
"I'm scared," I admitted, "Of the bombs."
"Yes, I know, but stay hopeful and someday they'll go."
"What can love do?"
"Love can do anything, and so can you!"

"So when the chances of winning the war seem low,
Believe in love and all the hate will go!"

Eleanor Pringle (8)

This Is Me

In a town where laughter is around,
A boy named Ned could be found,
He cherished the game of football, in his heart,
On the field, his eagerness will never depart.

With every kick, he conquers the pitch,
A warrior of grass, unmatched even with stitch,
The roar of the crowd, the rush in Ned's veins.
In the impressive stadium, he will break the chains.

But football alone did not define Ned's soul,
For food was his passion, not only scoring a goal.
From tacos to pies, he will whip up a feast.
A boy with a taste for the very best meats.

And when the game ended and all was set,
Ned loved his holidays, he'd never forget.
From a snowy Norfolk Christmas to the summer sun on his face,
Ned cherished moments, in every place.

So this is Ned, football's up-and-coming star,
Who likes to travel to places near and far,
With food for pleasure, he can find a way,
To have fun and enjoy life every day.

Ned English (11)

My Mum

She works, she works,
Hard as can be!
When things grow tough,
She's there for me.
She does the chores,
That to me are a bore,
They hurt her core,
And make her head roar
Even when she's sick,
She puts her head down,
And builds the bricks,
She makes sure she fixes the tea
Then goes to bed,
Tired as can be.
Sometimes she works long into the night,
I wake up and she gives me such a fright,
Long... long... into the night.
She makes my food,
She cooks the tea,
All day long,
Then she repeats

She plays with me,
Tries hard as can be,
But now I see,
Through her smiles of glee,
Sometimes she needs to sit down and enjoy her life,
Stuck with me
Ever since I was tiny,
She has cared for me kindly,
Even if I was sat there absent-mindedly.
Now as I grow older,
She can care for me like a boulder,
But now I see,
She will always be there for me

Daisy Rendle (11)

The Life Of Sam

They say
"Oh, Sam, why did you do that?"
"Sam, you're so annoying"
"Sam, stop it!"

And I think, *what?*

They say
"Sam, will you leave the dog alone?"
"Don't do it again, Sam"
"Sam, time out!"

And I think, *oh man*

But when I am helping people
by taking out their plates, they say
"Well done, Sam!"

When I play and stroke my puppy gently they say
"Thank you for being nice to the dog, Sam"

And when my teacher tells my mum
I have worked hard at school

She says
"Sam, I am really proud of you!"

I say
"How are you?" to the teacher in the corridor
I hold the door open for people sometimes
And I usually remember to say
"Please" and "Thank you"

I like being Sam because I am myself and I'm me!

Sam Lee (8)

A One And Only, Me!

If there was such a person who would change the world one day
Who would change the unjust ways we have unwillingly learned
From fear to acceptance, who would destroy evil

Does such a person exist?
Will paradise peace be kept one day?
Will the environment be perfect for once and for all?

Nobody knows, except the exact person who the selfless heroine is
We have all been waiting for
For the female, we have been waiting for
The leader, you see, is not a male but a rightful female

Why do our surnames come from our father, not our mother?
Why, even in modern times, does this brutal treatment of women continue? Why mankind, why not womenkind?

We are strong and brave, we are ferocious in battle,
Kind when needed, bold when unjust, fair and a female.
We should not be ashamed, we are what we are.

That's why, one little girl will speak up, for her rights...
Me!

Himavarsha Manchikanti (10)

Success And Failure

I've never been asked for my autograph,
I haven't made headlines or the news.
All my efforts seem in vain,
Days, weeks, months down the drain!

I haven't yet climbed the mountain of success,
I haven't yet won trophies or gotten awards,
I haven't anything to be proud of,
Nothing at all.

Yet still I try, bit by bit, to achieve;
Even when I fail, I still believe!
Working like a bee, I sting and shun my obstacles!
One day progress shall show, I know.

The fiery flame inside me shall never extinguish.
I will drill through mountains, claw through oceans,
Burn down forests that dare block my way,
I will show the world I'm forever unstoppable!

Fine. Perhaps burning forests is a bit wild.
I guess I'll stick to trying my best.
I'll definitely make the most of my life,
Even if I don't end up on front-page news!

Eddie Chen (9)

Life Goes On

Life...
Is...
Not the greatest.
Siblings are, okay?

But life still goes on
Just as normal
Or... at least as normal...
as it can be.

School was never the same after the incident.
My 'friends' changed,
And now I'm all alone
Being the victim.

But life still goes on
Just as normal
Or... at least as normal...
as it can be.

She was never like this
Mean...
Insulting...
Ignorant...

But life still goes on
Just as normal
Or... at least as normal...
As it can be.

Normally I see light through the darkness,
Hope through the doubt,
Love through the hate,
Friendliness even inside the cruellest of souls.

But now I no longer see:
The light of the morning sun,
The joy in the pain
The voice in the silence

I no longer see the friendliness in her eyes.

Mariana Abreu Fernandes (11)

This Is Me

My favourite food is spaghetti carbonara,
When it comes out all hot and steamy.
And the creamy taste of it makes my mouth want to water,
So delicious!

My favourite colour is turquoise,
It reminds me of the sea,
Gently foaming onto the golden sand.
As I sit on the beach.

My favourite season is winter,
When Christmas time draws near,
I enjoy going out shopping and spreading the cheer.
It's amazing when it's glittering frosty and fresh snow is on the ground.
But as I live in England, I never know when it will come.

I love to go swimming and explore the Earth's wonders,
The vibrant fish,
Turquoise waters
And the stark contrast of the sweltering, noisy beach
With the increasing peacefulness as I swim ever further.

I love to share this with you, to tell you who I am.
As we can be whoever we want in this world so very vast.

Chloë Grindal (11)

I Am Athena

I am Athena, goddess of war
And of wisdom most of all
My long hair almost hits the floor
I'm a writer and I can draw
I am happy, I am sad
I am anxious, I am mad
I'm mostly good but sometimes bad
But I'm perfect, says Mom and Dad
I'm sensitive and emotional
I have lots of friends, I'm social
I'm a YouTuber - I'm vocal
I have hundreds of subscribers in total
I have a condition called ADHD
It's a wonderful part of me
It makes me think differently
And have lots of energy
I'm good at editing and art
I'll dance when music starts
And I'll sing with all my heart
I'll act dramatically to every part
You're not just one thing, you're a lot

So, you can't be put in a box
So, be happy with what you've got
Because you're enough, don't think you're not.

Athena Christopher (10)

Ambition For Acceptance

I'm moving to secondary school!
I'm so excited
But I have worries too.
Will I make friends?
Will my grades show what I can do?
I'm scared that people won't like me.
Will my grades affect that?
If I get bad grades they'll call me dumb
But if I get the best they'll call me other names
Teacher's pet!
Show off!
How can I fit in if I'm not accepted for who I am?
I have to get grades lower than I'm capable of,
I have to be someone I'm not just to be accepted!
It's not fair!
So I won't care what they think
I'll do my best
I want to do my best
I like doing my best
I'm curious
I'm ambitious

I enjoy learning and seeing what I can do
So I'll do what I enjoy
Because I know that I'll meet people just like me,
People who will like me for who I am.

Grace Jarrett (11)

Your Mood

Your mood, my mood can be sunshine or a storm.
It has a way of changing your attitude every day,
Each day I look forward to having a nice sleep.
And wake up to see my lovely parent,
Seeing a lovely smile on their face brings out the sunshine in my mood.
Just going to school can be a happy feeling and a bad feeling,
A mix-up of feelings in my head,
But my sister gives me a cheer mostly with her lovely singing voice,
This sometimes makes the storm in my mood fly away,
And the sunshine coming to say hey!
Walking happily and jogging to school,
Seeing my teachers and assistant with a smile and saying,
Good morning and I walk to my friends, to see if they are happy.

I will tap them on the shoulder if they have a stormy mood,
And say it's going to be okay or just give them a hug.
This always ends my day with a jolly good smile.

Oluwanifemi Adejobi (8)

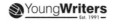

Who Am I?

This is me,
Javen, yes that's me,
Writing books at just ten years old,
Diving into poetry because I'm bold.

I'll put my name on the stage
Becoming big is my dream,
Writing books is what I like,
I hope to achieve.

Besides my hobby,
I'd like to go onto the medical side,
Studying and jotting down notes,
And taking some pride.

That's right, I want to become a doctor.
Treating patients and medical advice,
While I write as an author
I hope I'll thrive.

Even though my peers hate English,
I adore it very much
And it's the subject that I flourish.
Just keep on writing and then you'll clutch!

Well, that's me,
But remember.
Your life can be special too,
Just find your talent
And eventually, you'll have a clue!

Javen Matthew Colaco (10)

This Is Amelia

I like to eat, eat, eat,
I like to sleep, sleep, sleep.
I huggle and snuggle,
I ride and glide.
I'm not a fussy eater,
And I really like pizza.
I've got a chocolate Lab,
And a really cool dad
I love the sun with my crazy mum.
I've got an annoying brother,
That I like to call Bolyanner.
Don't forget the tortoise,
He is not very cautious.
I shade and I colour, I read and I write,
I like to think I'm very polite.
I always go to Spain to see my family,
So I'm always on a plane.
I'm a lover, not a fighter,
I'm loud and proud.
I make friends wherever I go,
And I will always have people I know.

I'm a dancer and prancer,
I've got blue and grey eyes, quite short hair,
You won't believe it when I say it but...

This is me!

Amelia Frappell (9)

What Do I Like?

Sometimes, I like running through the wind,
but other times I just want to sit down and relax,
and other times I want to go for a little jog.

Sometimes, I like challenging my friends at times tables,
but other times I just sit and just think slowly and get them correct,
and other times I'm stuck on a number, but I always push through.

Sometimes, I like looking through a telescope and seeing far-off galaxies,
but other times I just look at the sky
and other times I want to see if I can spot Mars first.

Sometimes, I read on and on and on,
but other times I would just like a break
and other times I just want to race and see who can read the Top Ten books first.

These are all things that I like,
I like them all, without a doubt, depending on how I feel,
but for sure, my favourite is my family and that never changes.

Finley Churchill (8)

This Is Me

Hi, my name is Jet-Leigh
There are so many things in the world that
I'd like to see
First of all, my friends call me Jet
Secondly, my mom won't let me have a pet
And thirdly, this is making me quite upset
Because this is something I'd really like to get
And fourthly, I don't like getting my hair wet

I don't like sprouts
They taste so bad inside my mouth
And I don't like cauliflower
Think I'd rather eat a flower
And spend all day in a hot shower

I love all things new
My favourite colour is blue
That's the colour of my shoe
I like to cover my hands in glue
And when it dries, I peel it off
That's what I like to do

I'm tall and slim
And I love to swim
And when my mom's not looking
I give my hair a trim.

Jet-Leigh O'Riordan (10)

An Amazing Recipe

To create a great Maxim you will need:
1kg of smartness.
200 grams of mischief.
3 boxes of Lego.
85% sport.
2 pinches of fun.
5 sprinkles of kindness.
4 dashes of curiosity.

Now you need to:
Boil the 2 pinches of fun at 100 degrees C
Then add 4 dashes of curiosity, next stir until
It bubbles. After that, one at a time, put in the
Five sprinkles of kindness. One box at a time, put
In the three boxes of clear blue Lego. Add on 85%
Of sport into the mixture, then wait until it cools
Down. After, pour in half of the 200 grams of mischief into the mixture,
Then after a minute pour the other half.
Just after, stir in the 1kg until it blends in with the mixture.

Finally, cook the mixture until it hardens. Then leave it to cool down.

This is me!

Maxim Johansson (8)

My Brother

(Hudson's brother has been diagnosed with autism and at first it was hard to understand)

My brother learns differently, he doesn't say hello
In fact, he's on repeat, "Ready set go!"
He doesn't answer questions with yes or please
He prefers to growl and do his ABCs.
He likes to watch Toy Story and Spider-Man,
He can recite them better than me, Mum or Dad can.
All he ever eats is toast,
Freezing cold is how he likes it the most.
I love it when he laughs at me
As soon as I say one... two... three...
But if I then say number four
He will just start head-butting the floor.
I really hope sometime he will ask me, "Do you want to play?"
Or maybe he will even answer, "How are you today?"

Until then we will keep running from monsters all around the place,
And then you can jump in your buggy because it's your safe space.

Hudson Lang (8)

This Is Me

This is me, this is me,
Full of hobbies,
This is what I do,
From creating and crafting,
Sticking and glueing,
Stitching and sewing,
Cooking with spoons
And brewing up stews,
This is me, this is me.

My future self is brimming with wealth,
A planned life of architecture,
A mighty dream,
Which will never wither
Like sweet steam,
A mighty idea,
Full of constructed wonders,
This is me, this is me.

Hobbies are my favourite,
Creativity is desperate,
Till my fingers twitch and hurt,
From the comfort of cooking,
To imagine and craft,
This is me, this is me.

I tickle him and her,
Make them laugh,
I am so much fun,
This is me, this is me.

Esther's full of empathy,
So funny,
Talented,
Helpful
Esther's got a clever strategy,
Ready to do anything,

Everything
It's her.

Esther Mbogol (10)

The Girl Who Had A Stroke

One day my life turned upside down,
There was a change in my smile and my frown.
My mum and doctors were really worried,
Blood tests, MRIs and CTs were hurried.

The doctors came in to talk to Mum and Dad,
I didn't know what was happening, but everyone seemed sad.
"You've had a stroke and there is damage forever on your brain,"
It was time to go to Southampton and have some drain.

There were some really scary times and things are still strange,
Nothing is quite the same and there has been a real change.
My mind works differently now and I have a wheelchair,
I'm taking things more slowly so my body can repair.

I'm still Ruby and I want to be the same,
I need to feel proud and not feel any shame.

Ruby Kingston (9)

This Is Me!

I could've been a prancing horse
That galloped speedily in a race;
I could've been a hopping hare
With an adorable, eye-catching face.

But no, I'm an amazing child!
This is great, this is me!
I grow, I learn, I play;
I'm who I'm meant to be!

I could've been a joyous fish
Swimming in the sea;
I could've been a paddling swan
As graceful as can be.

But no, I'm an astonishing dancer!
This is cool, this is me!
I jump, I twirl, I dance;
I'm who I'm meant to be!

I could've been a lime-green lizard
Crawling in the afternoon;
I could've been a brave, fearless wolf
Howling at the moon.

But no, I'm an incredible writer!
This is brilliant, this is me!
I read, I write, I create;
I'm who I'm meant to be!

Amelia Poon (8)

I Am So Glad To Be Me

Spectacular and clever me,
I am so glad to be me.

I am cheerful, I am kind,
Being helpful is always on my mind.

I like to visit lochs and castles,
My favourite fruit is mustard apples.

My favourite sports are swimming and football,
Which make me sharp, strong and tall.

Pink, amber and red are my favourite colours,
I watch Nat Geo to learn about
orcas and blubbers.

I laugh, I play, I enjoy my studies,
Mum and Dad are my best buddies.

I like my school, teachers and friends,
I read my storybook from start to end.

I'd eat cheeseburgers all day, I can't stop,
Followed by a brownie with ice cream on top.

Making myself only me,
Unique and exceptional me.

Shaily Mudholkar (7)

This Is Me

My name is Adil,
I enjoy jumping in puddles.
Football is my favourite game,
My aim is to have a lot of fame.
Another thing I like to do is gaming,
I find it very entertaining.
I have passion in my school,
It is very cool.
My best subject is maths,
I am extremely fast.
I love all my sports like swimming, karate and football,
I also do not mind basketball.
I really like baking,
It is completely amazing.
I play for Irvine Meadow,
And I enjoy a chocolate Freddo.
I am fond of cars,
With all those racing superstars.
I follow Islam,
It keeps me humble and calm.

I have great celebrations,
And have awesome communication.
There is loads more about me,
I am still growing like a tree.

Mohammed Adil Ahmad (10)

Every Day

Every day I wake up and say,
What are we going to do today?
Staying home to chill out,
Or getting up to go out and about.

If we go out it is always an adventure,
Visiting castles, going to fairs,
A day in London, Cambridge too,
Travelling by train, car or plane, it's always fun.

If the rain shows no mercy,
On days when it pours down the window,
Playing board or computer games,
It's always been fun.

Memories we'll always treasure,
Everywhere we go,
Each place has a special meaning,
And that will never change.

And every night we always say thanks,
To our parents who always try their best,
Who makes it fun, never boring,
And who is always there for us.

Charlotte Easter (11)

This Is Me!

Hi, I am Jasmine,
This poem is about me,
You should now read on.

I am 10 years old,
Just at the start of Year Six,
Sports captain and all.

My favourite subjects,
Are PE, history and art,
I like school a lot.

At home, I study,
Next to my sister, Ella,
We are always close.

I also live with,
My kind mother and father,
Who love me dearly.

I like to do sports,
I play county tennis now,
It is so much fun.

I'm a great athlete,
I really enjoy Sports Day,
It's like the Olympics.

I love nature,
My favourite colour is green,
I am creative.

Hi, I am Jasmine,
This poem is about me,
Thanks for reading.

Jasmine Koc (10)

Remember

When I think of you, all I see is your kind face and gentle smile
When I remember you, all I think of are the stories that will stay imprinted in my heart forever
As I look at photos, I realise that they only tell part of the story
As no picture could contain you in all your glory
I missed you before you were even gone
And if love could speak, it would say,
I'll help you to find the words you're trying to use
I'll remind you of things when you're lost and confused
Because although I knew you, I was often a stranger
But you'd remember you love me, sooner or later
So many memories, both happy and sad
But I have to remember, through the sorrow and pain
The happy memories will always remain.

Zoe Smaldon (11)

Your World Is Mine

Your world is mine and I'll tell you why.
They came close and looked into my eyes,
Then burst out in laughter, I tried not to cry.
They kept laughing for a long time, then I had it.
"Stop!" I yelled,
"Do you have any idea what you're doing?"
"No," they snickered.
"You're destroying the planet!"
There were puzzled looks on every face.
"You're meant to set an example for my future."
There was a pause.
After a while, they finally said,
"Sorry, we'll change our ways,
And make the future worthy days."
"Thank you," I said with a smile on my face,
"I'm sure it'll be a wonderful place."

Khadijah Miller-Nash (9)

This Is Me

I'm a very friendly and happy little prince
From the Tiv tribe in Benue state Nigeria.
I am hyperactive, full of energy and I love art.
I am very good with computers
I love my school and my friends.
I have a big sister, a mum and a dad.
I also have lots of cousins, aunties and uncles.
My dad is a doctor and my mum is a lawyer.
My big sister wants to be a doctor.
My grandad is the king and my grandma is the queen
Of the Tiv nation in Benue state Nigeria.
I want to be an artist when I grow up.
My hair is as black as the blackest of night.

- **S** aved to serve.
- **E** veryone matters to me.
- **F** riendly as can be.
- **A** cting responsibly is key to me.

Sefa Samuel Adura (9)

Who I Am

I am a boy called Stanley Brewster,
When I grow up, I want some Roosters,
I go to St Bartholomews,
Where we can play what we choose.

I was born on the 5th of June,
So, I get excited when it's soon,
I like eating blackberries,
And berries like that make me merry.

I like a Pokémon called Eevee,
I like them when they are near me,
I like playing on my Switch,
With games so good they make me itch

My pets include a dog,
Three cats, some fish but not a frog,
My cats and dogs have some toys,
Some squeak, some jingle and make some noise.

To do my best I do all I can,
And that's why I'm proud to say I am who I am.

Stanley Brewster (9)

Who Am I?

I wake with a start,
Quickly and silently; footsteps pad away.
A thief has stolen my memories, captured them,
locked them up,
Who am I?
My eyes wander about the room,
Not focusing on anything.
My brain is full,
About to burst.
Jammed, crammed,
Filled, stuffed.
Who am I?
Thoughts swirl around me blinding my vision,
Which are real, which are not?
Am I kind, am I mean?
Am I honest or am I dishonest?
Am I good, am I bad?
Am I humble or am I arrogant?
Who am I?
I blink,
In letters plastered on my wall, I read.

In case you forget...
You are amazing,
You are valued,
You are kind,
I smile to myself,
I know exactly who I am.

Pia Pradhan (11)

About Me

My name is Yusuf,
I am very tough.
I play lots of football,
Even though it can be rough.

I swim, run, and cycle,
I am very sporty,
I can be cheeky,
I try not to be naughty.

I dreamily doodle,
I love to read books,
My reading pace is as rapid as a cheetah,
I always get hooked!

The Quran is my holy book,
My religion is Islam,
I eat Halal food,
I must read Namaz.

I love a good adventure,
With lots of obstacles as well,
When I get back from one,
I have lots of tales to tell!

My hope is to be a footballer,
But also study too,
I am very passionate about science,
I might be a scientist and make goo!

Yusuf Rana (9)

This Is Me

I love being in the water,
Swimming like a sea lion,
Diving like an orca.
Surfing waves over head height,
Catching them, riding them to shore.

I love the outdoors,
Climbing ancient trees,
Rough bark under my hands.
Boating on the broads,
Birds, plants and nature comfort and surround me.

I love being in my bed,
Snuggling under the covers,
With Head-Ted and others.
Sister snuffling and shuffling in the bottom bunk,
like a little piglet.

I love stories,
Travelling back in the Time Machine,
Journeying to the Centre of the Earth.
Creeping along with Coraline,
Fighting the gorgon Medusa with Perseus.

This is me.

Robin Davies (8)

Who Can It Be?

His favourite sport is basketball.
But if you can't find him shooting hoops,
you'll find him playing football.
He has the cutest five-year-old brother,
And the most amazing father and mother.
His friends think he is very funny,
And he has an adorable pet bunny.
He is nine years old,
But sometimes he doesn't do what he is told.
He is trying to become an actor,
And he knows everything about a common factor.
His favourite TV show of all time is Friends,
But he doesn't like how the TV show ends.
He can play beautiful tunes
on a musical instrument,
And he cares about the environment.
Who can it be?

Answer: It's me!

Atlas Devrimoz (9)

Halloween

Spooky day and spooky night
Halloween is coming tonight
Children dress up for the night
That they might give a fright
Children knock on doors saying, "Trick-or-treat?"
As they meet while asking for some treats
Vampires and ghosts get their treats
When the full moon is up in the night sky
Like a ghost with no head, arms or feet
In the breeze, orange leaves fall off trees
And start dancing at their feet
Pumpkins are carved with different faces
And hollowed out before they are made
Adults and children place them by the door
And the pumpkins light up with horrific faces
Kids and adults have fun tonight
When the sun goes down at dawn of night.

Clinton Newman (8)

I Love Me

I am kind, caring and generous. Sometimes I can be a bit rebellious.

L oving others and animals is also what I do. When it comes to fashion, I love to pick and choose.

O f course, me being me, I love to care for nature. And I'm always wondering; what lives on the moon's crater?

V icious snakes and scorpions are what I'm scared of. But I'm not afraid of a gentle dove.

E xperimenting with food is what I do best. I'm a very good chef and I'll say it with my chest.

M ature behaviour is what I try to display. We all know it's not going to stay that way.

E njoying everything I get up to. My goal is to feed a kangaroo.

Aminah Badjan (11)

All About Me

I love music - rock, pop, all sorts,
My dream job is a singer and you can't change
my thoughts,
I really love cats, they're my favourite pet,
I do have a dog, not a cat just yet,
I love my dog like he is my brother,
I wouldn't accept it if they replaced him
with another,
I'm good at tennis and swimming too,
I like dancing and acting, how about you?
Olivia Rodrigo is my favourite singer,
Her amazing vocals made her a winner,
I live with my mum, my dog, my sister and my dad,
I love them so much when I'm happy or sad,
I hope you enjoyed my poem about me,
I wrote in other published books that are sadly
not free!

Vesta Ulozaite (9)

This Is Me, Nini

Playing football all day long,
Making goals until it's dawn.
Living life,
Being free.
This is me, Nini.

Hanging out with my siblings,
Brings me joy.
I'm filled with happiness,
Like a bright shooting star.
This is me, Nini.

Hanging out,
In the wind.
Car rides,
They are my favourite thing.
This is me, Nini

Toys, sand,
Mud, water,
These are the places you will mainly find me,
Being me.
This is me, Nini

I help my friends be happy,
Which puts a smile on my face.
The joy this brings me,
Knowing I made someone's day.

This is why I'm Nini.

Niniola-Gabriel Abayomi (7)

This Is Me

L ife of the party
U nique
C aring to family and others
I nterested in gaming
A lways happy
N inja is my future job

M usic is in my blood
O range juice is lovely
O nions are horrible
R iding a bike is fun
E li is my cousin's name

T he lead singer from The Drifters is my grandfather
H ome is my happy place
I have a little sister
S trawberries are my fave

I love to game
S witch is my gaming option

M oore is my family name
E nergy is something I never run out of.

Lucian Moore (6)

Poetry Is Me

Poetry Queen, coming towards your zone.
Stop me, and your heart will become stone.
I shine like a diamond, glisten bright like a star,
All the cats are following me, isn't it so bizarre?

Kicking the door, punching through all the walls,
I still hear muttering voices throughout the halls.
I sit to let my magical thoughts and dreams escape,
Snooping around quietly, wearing an invisible cape.

I write and write verse after verse, it fills me with joy,
Keeping me calm whilst living in the world we destroy.
Chose my path, packed my bags, I am all set and ready,
Storing my loved ones' love is my favourite teddy.

Farah Karim (10)

My Refuge Is My Home!

N ice and cosy is my home
O h my gosh! I love my home!

P erfect, perfect is my home
L ots of love in my home
A warm place is my home
C alm place is my home
E aster, Christmas and Diwali are celebrated in my home

L ots of respect in my home
I love my mummy's cooking in my home
K nock before you enter, I feel safe in my home
E shan is the best in my home!

H appy moments are made in my home
O h my gosh! I love my home!
M emories that last forever in my home
E at delicious food and sleep well in my home!

Eshan Pal (9)

This Is Me

I am cool,
I am smart,
If someone needs help,
I'll play my part.

This is me

I am kind,
I am caring,
I am careful,
But very daring.

This is me

Some people call me bossy,
But I don't care,
I wear cool clothes,
And have nice hair.

This is me

I have some favourite subjects,
English and PE,
When I spend time doing them,
It makes me happy and free.

This is me

I go to Cubs,
I am fast,
And in a race,
I'm never last.

This is me

I am nine years old,
I love reading,
I don't wear dresses,
I'm great at leading.

This is me.

Jessica Thorne (9)

Brown

I say I love the brown of my eyes,
Like deep pools of hazelnut chocolate.
"Blue eyes are better than brown," they say, such lies.
For this is me.

I say I love the brown of my hair,
Like fluffy, curly cotton candy.
"Blonde is better than brown," they say, don't they care?
For this is me.

I say I love the brown of my skin,
Like a calm, golden oasis.
"White skin is better than brown," they say, grinning.
For this is me.

I love the beautiful skin I'm in,
I don't care what anyone may think.
I slay all day, I am amazing within.
For this is me!

Alyssa-Grace Harriette (11)

My Silly Face!

As electrified as a free orangutan
My hairy brown ears are a searing frying pan
Like two connecting rusty cans
It makes me look like a hilarious old man

As black as joyful ants
My ebony eyes are shaped like stripy pants
Moving drunkenly like a waving tree
It makes me look like a buzzing bumblebee

As bouncy as a couch
My button nose is a muddy pig's snout
Around the coffee-caramelised swamp
It makes me look like a lumpy trump

As wide as a rocky grey floor
My opening-closing mouth is a broken door
A bitterness coats my addicted tongue
Every time I munch my teeth go numb.

Starlar Ho (8)

This Is Me

I am a boy who loves maths, reading and football,
I am a boy who's curious, smart and tall,
I love to solve problems, read books and play,
And I do it all with passion every day,

I spend hours on math problems, never giving up,
And I'll read books for hours, rarely cleaning up,
I'll play football with friends, never losing my cool,
And usually, I score goals with ease, never breaking a rule,

I am a boy who's kind, caring and true,
And I'll always be there to help you through.
I am a boy who loves maths, reading and football,
A boy who's special, unique and stands tall.

Shaylan Somal (10)

I Love The Beach

I love the sun blazing when I'm at the beach.
Especially, when the tide is in reach,

Kids make sandcastles, and have so much fun,
And pleasingly watch the sand fall from their hand, until it's all done.

People happily swim in the pretty ocean,
They skim stones to see who will get the most jumps
But some relax in the honey-glowing sun,

People lay down their towels by the bay,
And watch the tide sway,

People go surfing high and low,
Volleyball time, come on, let's go,

Go eat a picnic, food galore,
Get out of your seat as there's a beach to explore!

Esmae Emin-Wyatt (10)

Recipe Of Me

Take two legs and arms,
Throw them in the pot, leave to brew,
Blend in a sprinkle of freckles,
A creative spark,
And a couple of eagle eyes,
Drizzle in some slothiness.

Boil up some anger,
Stand well back!
Dollop a drop of fury,
Then stir thoroughly.

Pour in some compassion,
Add five pinches of honesty,
A couple of ounces of kindness,
250 grams of gratitude and a large jar of memories.

Heat till bubbling, then leave to cool,
Splatter on some ferocity and a dozen pots of modesty,
Wait ten years for it to grow,

There you have it,
A liberty!
Liberty Bridges (10)

This Is Me

This is me
This is me, I am unique.
This is me, I am different
This is me, I am not the same
You are you
I am myself
We are different
This is me
I am different
This is me
I am not you
You are not me
It's okay if you're different
This is me
This is my poem
You have yours
Mine is different
Because we are unique
I might win stuff
You might not

This is because
This is me!
I have glasses
You might not
That doesn't matter
Though...
This is me
I might be younger than you but still...
This is me!

Nyla Kabir (7)

This Is Me

M y name is Maariya Bhamji
A nd I come from a wonderful family
A lso there is something I want to tell you
R ight now, so please don't boo
I am kind but can be mean
Y ou can say that I'm nearly a teen
A s I am going to turn eleven

B esides, my brother is just over seven
H ello is what I try to remember to say wherever I go
A nd sometimes I try to impress people but not with fancy clothes or a bow
M aybe I can be a little frustrating
J ust sometimes I'll be joking
I think I am okay at being a poet.

Maariya Bhamji (10)

My Life Is Fun!

Hi, my life is so much fun!
I have 21 first cousins and a lot of friends,
I am in love with Stitch,
I love animals too,
Every time my cousins have a party,
It is always water fights, slip and slide, bouncy castles with Fairy Liquid,
It is so fun, I have the best time,
They take me with them,
I've been to bouncy castles, water parks, and loads more,
They are in love with all my cute little pets,
All 24 love them all,
I have pets!
How I look:
I have blonde curly hair, blue eyes and glasses,
I am very silly, brave, chatty, adventurous, funny, sporty, and happy!
This is me!

Faye Convery (9)

This Is William, This Is Me

I am William and I am nine,
My favourite thing to do is art and design.

I play on my Xbox morning and night,
When I was two, I enjoyed flying a kite!

I love to eat burgers with a chocolate milkshake,
For my dessert, I eat blue banana ice cream with a sprinkle of flake!

Basketball and football are my favourite sports to play,
I'm practising my shooting because I want to be the best, okay?

Times tables are easy for me to learn in class,
If I had a test, I think I would pass.

I am William and I am kind,
If you need a friend, I am always there to find!

William Thompson (9)

Free

Screaming and crying,
I struggle to get free,
Sick of trying,
I flail helplessly.

A civil war between my mind,
Hopes and dreams go to waste,
Discarded like some lemon rind,
Yet my bitter pain, I cannot taste.

Slowly, I see some shining light,
Golden and celestial against the obsidian-black night,
Of course! Why couldn't I spot it before?
There are friends and family to help me galore.

I heave myself out of the deep ravine,
And realise I am finally free,
Free as a butterfly,
Swooping and diving as I say goodbye.

Free.

Kangti Li (10)

This Is Sky!

To make me, you will need:

A pizza
35 grams of curiosity
2 tablespoons of reading
A gallon of fries
A sprinkle of TV
A pinch of board games
A teaspoon of holiday
A bowl of kindness
2 cups of helpfulness
A gram of stubbornness.

Now, what you do is:

Mix the kindness, helpfulness, and curiosity so it makes a blue liquid.
Put the stubbornness in.
Mix the holiday, board games, and TV so they make a yellow liquid.
Put the fries in.

Place both the liquids in a tray and bake for 20 minutes.
Put the pizza on top.
Leave to cool.

Sky Kwok (9)

This Is Me

I'm as calm as a river,
Wise as an owl,
I'm as fast as a cheetah,
As daring as an arrow,
I'm as kind as a friend,
Who helps you every day,
I'm that kind of person,
In every single way,
I've been broken down,
Then built back up,
Life sends massive ripples,
Like tea in a teacup,
I'm as colourful as a parrot,
Positive as a plus,
As tall as a mountain,
And as beautiful as dusk,
In my story writing,
My wings are beginning to unfurl
A phrase to describe me,
Is 'a lovely, smart girl'
I'm as creative as an author,

As you can see,
I'm writing this poem,
And this is me.

Rita Krasnici (9)

This Is Me!

I am Shreeya, I am kind
This is very hard to find.
A generous girl I am
Who helps anyone in no time.

I respect my teachers
And I love my school
I have many friends whom
I play with, who think I'm cool.

I love all sports
Netball, gymnastics and swimming
I can't stop my passion -
My passion for winning!

I like running
I like drawing
I like painting
I use my imagination.

I love my mum,
I love my dad

But most of all, my sister is my favourite
I am nothing without my wonderful, caring family.

Shreeya Arora (8)

Do You Know?

I am a celebrity,
But what is my name?
In lockdown, I gave online free live sessions to children
(Who I must not name)
Thirty-five is my age
And you can learn more about me on my webpage
I won the BAFTA award in 2017 for children
Do you know how a water slide works?
Do you know how Lego is made?
Are my specialities
I know everything about science,
From a giraffe's neck to a beetle foot
I am an author and write science books
On stage, I have battled against Captain Hook
So now think
Do you know who I am?

Answer: Maddie Moate.

Oujj Shah (11)

My Name Is Hec

My name is Hec
And last time I checked
I had about a hundred pets or more
I love all creatures
But don't tell the teachers
I sometimes bring them to school

My fav is our dog called Miss Moss
Though we tell her the rules
She ain't no fool
And goes with what's cool
Because she's really the boss
Then there's my gecko named Cresty
Who's also my bestie
He lives in a tank on my floor
When we let him out
He'll zoom about
Then jump straight out of the door!

I've newts in my boots and bats in the curtains
But what's certainly certain
Is I'm always looking for more!

Hector Gathorne-Hardy (9)

This Is Me!

Who am I?
I am me!
Over the hills,
And over the seas,
There is no one like me.
Sometimes rough, funny and kind
With loads of questions in my mind.

So, over the hills,
And over the seas,
There is no one like me.
My favourite book is Harry Potter,
While the temperatures get hotter,
Black, inky hair and small, elegant eyes,
There is nothing in me that I defy.

As you can see, over the hills,
And over the seas,
There is no one like me.
Nobody's the same,
No one is to blame,

So, you can see,
I am me!

Shravya Shrivastava (10)

Me, Only Me

I used to think of myself as lifeless, terribly dull and boring,
I used to think of myself as quiet, afraid to go exploring,
I used to think of myself as a bird, afraid to go flying,
I used to think of myself as irrelevant, always lying,
I used to think of myself as caged, the opposite of free,
I used to think of myself as the opposite of me,

I now think of myself as growing, with a great mind,
I think of myself as happy, spirited and kind,
I think of myself as settled, calm and free,
I think of myself as me, only me.
Me, only me.

Lily Ingrey-Counter (11)

What Makes Me, Me

I'm far away, drifting on a cloud of imagination.
For once in a while, I'm doing something different.
I'm free but trapped in a bubble of sorrow.
I'm alone but I have company deep inside me...
I'm magical but normal.
I have the speed of a cheetah and the speed of a tortoise.
I have the strength of a rhino and the strength of an otter.
I have the intelligence of an orca and the stupidity of an ant.
I'm riding on a constellation of stars surrounded by the universe.
I am burning like a lit fire and freezing like a winter's puddle.

Connie Farley-Hills (7)

This Is Me, Magnificent Mishka

Marvellous Mishka, that's me,
I eagerly go to Shaftesbury Primary School.
Spreading love with a smile, sharing and caring to all I meet,
Helpful, hopeful and kind is my style when people struggle, making life so sweet.
Kindness and laughter with my friends give me joy,
Appreciate life, and stay elated and bright.
I'm seven years old, happy as can be,
My favourite colour is blue, as far as I can see
And I grow with my friends in a joyful crew.
I feel royal and bake wraps in a piece of foil.
I try my best and I am Mishka, the best in the rest.

Mishka Saxena (7)

I Am A Rock Star!

Brave and kind, I try to find,
But angry is mad and buzzy,
Sometimes, I'm just very fuzzy,
Happy jumps like a bouncy ball,
I stand tall because
I am a rock star!
I giggle, I wiggle, I fiddle,
Sometimes, I just piddle,
I scream at the shadows when I'm sleeping,
I'm scared of the dark when it's creeping,
I stand tall because
I am a rock star!
If I was a glue stick,
I would glue my sad to my feet,
So that I can stomp and stamp,
And leave it in some street,
I stand tall because
I am a rock star!

Lilly Rai Hardey (6)

Hopes And Dreams

If happiness is what you want,
Follow your own path.
Every day, try smiling,
Or turn around and laugh.

If success is in your mind,
Listen to me here.
Never go and follow what is called
The drill of fear.

If forgiveness is the thing you crave,
Follow Jesus' way.
If someone makes you feel sad,
Say to them, "It is okay."

If knowledge is the thing you need,
Do what I now say.
Listen to your teachers well,
But leave some time to play.

If happiness is what you want,
Follow your own path.
Every day, try smiling,
Or turn around and laugh.

Melina-Rose Papalambrou (9)

Me

I am Lucy, kind, happy and helpful
My love of learning opens doors to becoming a surgeon
Reading is great, it lets my mind relax
Playing the piano is wondrous,
It takes me to many magical places.

Musical theatre brings light to dark places in me
Swimming in the pool and racing pushes me to do my best
Cuddling my guinea pigs brings out my compassionate and caring side
Being crafty stretches my mind.

I love my family they bring joy to my heart
I am grateful for all those who support me
They encourage me, to be the best me.

Lucy Davies

Rockets Go Boom

Rockets go boom, balloons go pop.
My heart goes pound, space goes bang!

Nintendo Switches go click,
and phones go ding.

Rockets go boom, space goes bang,
and my heart goes pound.

Dragons are cool, they breathe fire.
Galaxies form like my deepest anger.

My happiness forms like a star,
and shines brightly like a blood moon diamond.

I like monkeys, and rabbits too,
hopping and swinging from planet to planet.

Ice cream is super yummy and so tasty, yum!
It will blow your universe away!

Harvey John Morton (9)

Sebastian

S wimming is my favourite activity, I practise professionally
E ntertaining, I always make my friends laugh or smile
B oating is a thing I like to do, especially in rowing boats
A thletic, I have joined a lot of swimming competitions
S leepy, I sleep a lot when it is the weekends
T ime, I usually waste time playing video games
I dols, I have a lot of idols, most of them are world-class swimmers
A ttracted by holidays and days off school
N egative, sometimes I am negative about dangerous things.

Sebastian Mihai (10)

This Is Me Josiah

This is me Josiah and I am seven years old and a twin as well.
I am fun, lovely and jovial.
I like playing tricks on my siblings.
I like playing football, hide-and-seek.
I am also good at swimming.
My favourite food is a hot dog with apple or orange juice.
My favourite animal is a dog.
I am good at times tables and spellings.
I like playing drums with pencils.
I like going to the woods with my family to explore.
I like running and jumping.
I really like history and like reading about Neil Armstrong.
This is a bit about me.

Josiah Amoah (7)

This Is Me

E nthusiastic about life's journey
N is for noble, clever and kind
T is for truthful, truthful to the core
H is for happiness, the smile I bring
U is for unique, no one is like me
S is for sophistication that reflects your style
I is for independent like me
A is for awesome, I do what I enjoy
S is for special, I simply amaze
T is for trusting, intelligent and smart
I is for interesting, fascinating to talk to
C is for creative, always a joy.

Raeesah Khan (10)

My Mind

All noise fades as I enter my mind
Not a sound to be heard
I think of all things kind
Soaring through my head like a beautiful bird

I see a majestic story, a story that tells
Of anger, shame and fear
And in my eye, it wells
I shed a single tear

The smells that dance around me
The scents so sweet, I have to appeal
Smells of sugar and tea
Candies of red, yellow and teal

My mind is hard at work
Crafting nightmares and dreams
In my subconscious, they lurk
With imagination, my mind teems.

Joshua Ahmed (10)

Friendship

F riends are the family you choose and make
R espect and relying on one another brought you together
I ndeed, every person is different and unique
E very acceptance comes from the heart of friendship
N ote that everyone deserves a chance to join
D epend on each other to help you along the way
S tick up for everyone
H elp friends whenever you have the chance
I n life, you will always cherish memories that were made on the way
P atience is accepting one another for being slow.

Maria Miah (11)

All About Me

Oi... Oi...
I am a good boy
Who plays with toys
I play with different types of balls
My favourite sport is football
I want to grow tall
I don't like going to the mall
My school assembly happens in the hall

My favourite England team is Liverpool
I have lots of tools
Be careful, I am not a fool
Because I am cool
I go to Mayville Primary School

I am smart
I sometimes fart
I like doing lots of art,
My favourite dessert is custard tart
Now, go to the top and read from the start!

Muhammed Zeshan Aariz Wehvaria (8)

Seasons

In spring, the leaves on the tree are a bright, blinding green
With blossoms, pink blossoms dangling off the branches

In summer, the buds open on the tips of twigs
With bees, buzzing bees visiting the nectar

In autumn, the leaves start to fall
With children, playful children kicking them in the air

In winter, the tree lies bare
With snow, settling snow collecting on the branches

But in all of the seasons, I think trees are beautiful
With all the changes that they go through

Just like me.

Jeeva Jandu (8)

An Introduction To Myself

I am tall, I am fair
I meet people and don't really care
How they were, how they look
I am a reader and love a lot of books.
Biographies, dictionaries, a guide to cooking
These are books at which I won't ever be looking.

Caring am I, I am sweet
You will not expect me to cheat.
Dark is my skin, same as my hair.
I love little, cute, cuddly bears.

Nine is my age, soon to be ten.
Though I'd like to be six again
Family of five, lucky I'm alive
One of my fears is buzzy beehives.

Michelle Akadiri (9)

This Is Me

The colour pink, the season of fall,
The word create, and most of all,
The flavour of sweet, the weather warm,
This is me.

The quote 'good vibes' and butterflies,
This is me.

I read and write,
I sing and act,
I draw and design too.

To change the world, this simple fact,
It starts with me and you.

I am what I say I am,
And you are who you are.

These words do not define 'me'
But give you an idea,
Of who I am
And who I try to be.

Charley Biereth-Purcell

Simply Me

Cerebral palsy is a part of me,
But I won't let it defeat me.
I face challenges every day,
But I find the strength to push it away.

I may stumble and I may fall,
But I get up and stand tall.
Cerebral palsy is part of me
But it doesn't define that I'm simply me.

Simply me is amazing to be
And I won't stop being different because of other people's authority.

I have pride in my disability
And I hope tomorrow it will become an ability
By being simply me.

Daisy Campbell (9)

This Is Me

This is me
An angelic boy
With a face full of glee
As shiny as a coin.

This is me
Equipped with a diligent brain
I will overcome it all
Sun, wind, and rain.

This is me
I have lots of talent
Yet my incomplete life
Is equally balanced.

This is me
An ideal spot for hugs
After a challenging day at school
We'll be snuggling on the rug.

This is me
A very comedic friend
But I'm very sorry to say
That this poem has come to an end.

Sacha Kasmi (11)

This Is Me, Just Me

This is me,
Just me,
Special,
And unique.

The food I eat,
Is gluten-free,
Because I have,
An autoimmune disease.

I have a massive imagination
Full of magical things
With fantasy fairy tales
And queens and kings.

Pandas are my favourite animal,
But I like others too,
Everyone is different from one another,
From what we say to what we do.

'Cause this is me,
Just me,

Not just the same as anyone else
Just what I believe.

Hannah Roper (10)

This Is About Me

I love to read exciting books,
Books full of adventure!
I feel happy and calm when I am snuggled in my book corner.
Stories are full of fun, like a roller-coaster ride!
I love to explore the woods.
Where's the teddy hiding?
Do you want to play hide-and-seek?
Collecting corns and conkers under the tree
Not far from the school.
It's quiet and relaxing in the woods.
I love to walk, swim and play netball
Climb trees all the way to the top
Reading and art are my thing
I am always kind and caring, if you know me
Sipping strawberry smoothies.

Isobel Sloan (7)

Love For My Family

L ovely
O h, so crazy
V ery close
E merald is my house colour at school

F unny
O n time never (sometimes)
R eally fun

M y mum's favourite food is lasagne
Y ellow is my mum's favourite colour

F amily are
A nnoying (some of them)
M ade to love
I like my mum and sister best
L ike really caring
Y es, they're annoying but I will always like them (some of them).

Alice Walton (9)

A Recipe For Me!

For this recipe you will need:
A flake of foodie
A pint of sportiness
A cup of quirkiness
A spoon of smart
A slurp of fun
And a mug of football fan

First, pour in the cup of quirkiness
Then stir with a spoon of smart
Then, add a slurp of fun and stir it again
Add a pint of sportiness and a mug of football fan
After that, spread it out on a baking tray
Bake at 350 degrees Celsius for 15 minutes
Finally, sprinkle with a flake of foodie!

This is a recipe for me!

Brandon Tailor-Hooker (11)

This Is Me - An Artist

My name is Nikolas and I love to make art.
This is something that emerges from the
bottom of my heart.
When I paint, I feel calm,
Like a baby in a pram.
I love sketching and colour mixing,
But don't ask me how I'm fixing,
The errors paints make,
When they crack and flake.
I'm a realist in style,
And I find it worthwhile,
Taking pictures of what I see,
And, on my paper, setting them free.
Through my art everything I see,
Becomes the best it can ever be.

Nikolas Kornelakis (8)

This Is Me

This is me,
No one can change that,
I struggle a lot,
People know me as 'liar girl',
Or 'fat girl',
No comments can change who I am,
I am me,
This is my story to tell, no one else's,
I am passionate about writing,
I am not a nerd,
I am not a geek,
I am a proud 12-year-old girl who made it,
I struggle a lot mentally,
Writing lets me express how I feel,
I like writing,
I like reading,
No one can stop me,
'Cause I am me.

Grace Ash (12)

I Am Me

I am me and you are you,
Life goes on and on,
I am silly and fun too,
Can I speak French? Oui!

I am messy and I am kind,
I really do love reading,
Look at me closely and you will find,
A smile dancing in my eyes,

I'm a good dancer,
I love a song,
I'm sometimes a mess at my maths,
I'm really quite hopeless at not smiling,

Sometimes I feel like I don't belong,
But next minute my heart is roaring in song.

Skye Tallowin (8)

Unique Me

U nique, I am one-of-a-kind
N ever give up and always determined
I nventive, full of surprises
Q uerist, with questions of all sizes
U nderstanding of thoughts and feelings
E nergetic, active and non-stop speaking

M annerly, organised in all ways
A rtistic, creative in many ways
N ever-ending fun, just a delight
H elpful, honest and polite
A mbitious reader and loves to write.

Manha Abdullah (10)

This Is Who I Am

I am a girl with passion,
A girl with love.

A girl who loves fashion
And a girl as nice as a dove.

I may be a normal girl
But beneath lies an adventurous whirl

With a heart of fire,
Personality so sweet,
Chocolates my desire
It's so lovely to eat!

I love my best friends
I like making them laugh,
If someone's done something to them,
I'm there to defend,
As a joke, they call me a giraffe!

Khadija Aktar (11)

Happiness

Sometimes you are not that happy
But when that time comes
Be happy and cherish your life
Be open to criticism
And take that chance to grow and learn
Action may not bring happiness
But there is no happiness without action

Happiness depends upon us
The time that you use
To do something that you enjoy
Is not wasted time
Turn someone's frown upside down
With one kind word
One kind word can mean
The world to one person.

Ryan Haque (9)

My Family

Family is the best.
They help you when you are down,
And make sure that, on your face, there
is never a frown,
Mums, dads, brothers and sisters,
No matter if you only have one or two,
They are and will always be there for you.
I love my family.
I'm sure that even after a big fight,
We will always live happily.
Every family is different in all sorts of ways,
But there is one thing they all have in common,
And that one thing is love.

Sarah Tossou Gbete (10)

This Is Me And I Am Alia

I am Alia

And this is all about me.
Music is my jam I love to play the violin, it's my favourite instrument.

Amusing as it seems I can't tell the difference about what colour my eyes are -
Are they brown or are they emerald-green?

LP is my brother and FK is my sister, they can be annoying but funny,
Either way, I love them lots.

I love my family and my friends; we have fun every day.

And this is me!

Alia McWilliams (10)

The Things I Adore

These are things that I adore,
I love football, food and much more.
I love football because it's fun to play.
I can play it every day.
I love whoever invented chips
I love chips when they touch my lips.
When I am thirsty, I love to drink
I never ever pour it down the sink.
Now I am going to tell you my favourite thing
It is wrestlers brawling in the ring.
Even though some are bigger and meaner
No one is better than John Cena!

Hartley Taylor-Richardson (8)

Reading

R eading is what I love to do, I am never without a book
E very day I learn something new, books are amazing
A uthors just amaze me; they're so talented, intelligent and imaginative
D ahl, Darwin and David Walliams, I love them all
I gniting my imagination, letting it run wild
N o TV, PCs or consoles for me, just give me a book and set my mind free
G reat novels, great authors, what is there not to love?

Issabelle Ord (9)

This Is Me

S tars shine bright like the sun in the sky
H owever, I am the brightest and shiniest star of all time!
A pples and oranges are my favourite fruit to eat
H owever, in competitions, I am the one to beat!
N ot forgetting to mention, I always love a hug
O h, but the thing I hate the most are bugs!
O ne dream of mine is to be the greatest doctor of all
R eady to help people at their beck and call.

Shahnoor Zahra Khan (5)

I Love Cats

C ats are what I love and cats are what I like.
H uddled together in the night, but if you trip over them you'll get quite a fright.
A lways purring in the sunshine, pattering down the stairs.
R eady for some mischief.
L eaping everywhere.
O range and cream, grey and white, with splashes of black in-between.
T hunder of paws,
T ossing their toys,
E very cat is a treasure to me.

Charlotte Sugden (8)

Poem All About Me

This is a poem all about me,
It is about things I will treasure and things that
I despise.
My favourite colour is brilliant blue,
You often see me drawing but I love to read too.

I have a cat, her name is Sky,
And when she pounces around she thinks she
can fly.

I dislike technology,
Therefore if there was a drawing I would enjoy
it more.

And that is a poem all about me,
Made by Imogen Cobley.

Imogen Cobley (11)

This Is Me!

I am a Lego master,
I play for hours a day
I have thousands of pieces
And I build my own way.

I am good at coding
I have already created a game
I have lots of drafts,
But they're never the same.

I have a love of Pokémon
I have over a hundred cards
My favourite is Regice,
He shoots ice shards.

I do a lot of reading
My favourite's Gangsta Granny
With a fun tale and weird laughs,
It truly is uncanny!

This is me!

Aarav Dhiman (9)

Rainbow Ride

Over the rainbow, I see my dreams
Over the rainbow is not as far as it seems
I love many colours
My favourites are yellow, purple and blue
Come help me find my dress and some pretty shoes.

If my dress is yellow, then my shoes should be blue
That only leaves purple
I want that in there too
A purple bow or a purple cape?
It's so hard to decide
I just grabbed my purple something
And went on my Rainbow Ride.

Summayyah Hoque (8)

This Is Me

A nother thing about me
U niquely different to others
T ired of hurting other people's feelings
I try so hard to stop, but I just can't
S ometimes, I get angry with myself about it
T he masking in me brings me such joy, but also brings me such misery and makes me not able to breathe.
I find labels and loud noises are difficult for me.
C hange hurts my brain, and causes me pain.

Orla Hamilton (10)

Best Of Me

I'm a curious little fox,
In a little box
Ready to unbox
My gifts and talents.
I'm a swift-moving dolphin
Gliding and diving.
People praise how I sing.
They think I'm the next Elvis.
I'm as good as a rat, playing dead.
You might see me,
On the big screen one day.
I'm sensational when it comes to gaming.
People say I'm very kind and caring.
This includes my family, friends and teachers.
"Yes," it is true.

Evan Senanayake (10)

This Is Me

Dear Diary,
16/09/2023
This is me
I am done hiding in the shadows
This is me
I am who I am
This is me
I am my own person
This is me
I don't take other people's complaints
This is me
I make my own rules
This is me
I don't need your opinions
This is me
I don't need anyone's support
This is me
I am my own queen
This is me
I love me
Gurmeen.

Gurmeen Kaur (11)

Lonely

L ove is all I need but all I see is greed.
O nly my imagination keeps me company in the playground.
N ever ever have I felt so lonely and even in class I slowly fade away.
E nd this loneliness and please let school feel homely.
L aughter, smiles, giggles are now in my dreams. Please don't let me wake up to scream.
Y elling is all I feel like doing but telling I think will make things worse.

Nevaeh Pancholi (7)

What Is The ZoZo Way?

What is the ZoZo way?
It takes a bit of energy and a bit of skill,
Now, don't forget the flexibility or you'll stay still.
You can see me hanging on the monkey bars,
Or climbing like a chimpanzee.

But that is not all ZoZo can do, she can split like the sea,
Move aside as she cartwheels like a little pea.
That is the ZoZo way, come join us for tea,
We'll have fun, you see.
Shall we?

Zoya Iqbal

A Little Bit About Me

I am Jeremiah and I am 7 years old and a twin.
I am good at maths, especially times tables.
My favourite subject is history and I really enjoy watching Neil Armstrong's first landing on the moon.
I like doing spellings.
My favourite animal is a dog.
I really enjoy going to the beach with my family to have fun during the summer holidays.
I am a Manchester United fan and I like playing football.
This is me.

Jeremiah Amoah (7)

This Is Me...!

My name is Sargam,
I'm bubbly as a bubblegum
I always go to school,
But I wish I could spend more time in the swimming pool
I'm kind, respectful, funny and caring,
Sometimes I'm playful and sometimes I'm boring
I love going to the park,
But not when all dogs bark
I wish I was a vet
And have every animal as my pet
I no longer wish for princesses and unicorns,
But slime, L.O.L.s and Lego are what I want.

Sargam Shrotri (7)

This Is Me

J oyful
A mazing
K ind boy
E xcellent at maths

B rilliant blue eyes
R eally good at PE
Z en, which means very relaxed
E legant and smart
Z ippy, which means energetic
I ncredible
N ice and sweet
S uper good friend
K ing of grumpiness sometimes
I love food, especially sausage and mash.

Jake Brzezinski (6)

I Am Roberta

R adiant and resourceful
O ptimistic and outstanding
B reathtaking and brave
E ager, extraordinary and enthusiastic
R espectful and robust
T alented and tender-hearted
A n angel who dropped out of heaven

H umble, honest and helpful
U nforgettable and unique
H ardworking and high-spirited
N oble and nice, this is me.

Roberta Huhn (11)

The Perfect Friend

The perfect friend is not a liar,
His pants are not on fire.
The perfect friend is not pessimistic,
His outlook is more realistic.

The perfect friend is not a bully,
He loves everyone equally.
The perfect friend does not put on an act,
He is much more matter-of-fact.

The best of friends is not perfect,
Knowing him is much more worth it!
The best of friends is not perfect,
But then neither am I!

James Bass (10)

All About Me

T ime is fun when I get to write,
H owever, I'm quite small in my height.
I t may be fun and it may be sad,
S till, I love everyone when I'm mad.

I love being a poet and maybe a story writer too,
S ending out my poems might be a bit new.

M inding my own business can be a bit hard,
E asily, it's very hard while doing art.

Erick Karim (8)

Me, Myself And I

D azzling brain, the smartest of all,
O verly towering, you would love to be so tall.
R adiant personality, hilarious and kind,
I ntelligent brain and intelligent mind.
N aturally persistent, I need to please everyone.
D aring and adventurous, though I get a bit scared,
A little bit too proud... we don't talk about that, as if anyone cared!

Victoria-Dorinda Ametefe (10)

What I Feel

I got the pain,
It left a stain,
I went insane,
I left my reign,
But it caused me to rain,
And now I feel this overwhelming pain,
I mean, it is in my veins,
I mean, it is in my brain,
Like toy rain,
This is just the price I have to pay,
How can this overwhelming pain go away?
Pain is pain, it never goes away,
It stays in one place and never goes away.

Zahra Mukhtar Zia (10)

Icy Ice Cream

Ice cream, the most delicious dessert,
After dinner, I ask my mum, "Can I have ice cream, please?"
But I also make sure my sister has it first,
Summer is my favourite time of year to eat ice cream because it cools me down!
Vanilla is my number one flavour,
Especially on a cone with a flake and chocolate sauce oozing around it,
But watch out for brain freeze!

Sarwan Bains (8)

Sleeping At Night

When I try to sleep at night
Not everything feels alright

Unwanted thoughts go through my head
Always thinking about the things ahead

It never has a start or an end
Like a letter, I can never send

But I always have a little plan
But I can never understand

When I wake up it's all fine
And I realise I've just turned nine.

Charlotte Holmes (9)

My Name Is Cristina

C ould I tell you a little bit about me?
R eading is my calming key
I am a librarian, can't you see?
S traight brown hair, dark brown eyes
T ell everyone unicorns are my life
I really hope you enjoy this poem
N ow it's almost done
A nd don't forget to leave the room in your day for lots and lots of fun!

Cristina Alvanos (10)

I Am Not ADHD

I wake up in the morning
And what do I see,
Just a little boy with ADHD...
I'm crazy, they say, or stupid you see
But I know I'm not
I'm just a boy with ADHD.

I'm clever, I'm smart and I'm funny too...
But all they see is a boy with ADHD.

I may be young but I know who I am
I'm not just the boy with ADHD.

Corey James Clark (9)

Terrific Thunderstorm

Crash!
Went the scary lightning in a rage,
Whilst the thunder was locked in a fiery cage,
When the thunder was punching the ground,
The soggy buildings made a crashing sound.
The thunderstorm is a mass of flames,
That likes playing wonderful games,
Not fun, exciting games,
They are frightful games,
That will leave you in burning flames.

Malaika Gumbo (9)

My Happy Place

The fire was lit on the beach,
Waves crashing on the shore,
Dolphins swimming in the distance,
And the gentle crackle of burning wood.
The moon reflected on the sea,
Whilst stars twinkled in the sky.
Palm trees danced in the gentle breeze,
The nearest town to the beach was silent,
Every animal asleep,
And what a peaceful night it was.

Paige Graham (10)

This Is Me

I am the boy who
Plays football every single day of the week,
I am the boy who
Loves his guinea pigs who squeak,
I am the boy who
Loves his friends and family who care,
I am the boy known
For his blonde curly hair,
I am the boy who
Is captain of his school football team,
I am the boy who
Loves a good chocolate ice cream.

Jacob Payne (10)

Harvest

H ay as yellow as a star in the night sky
A utumn as cold as the North Pole
R ed bouncy balls falling from the trees
V egetables breaking free from their dirty abode
E dible orange swords stuck in the ground
S weetcorn as yellow as a chick
T rees as tall as mountains

It's harvest time.

Lucas Varney (9)

My Nature Friends

I like sunshine,
But my sun is shy.
I love such weather,
When we walk together.

When I look around,
I see a nice mount.
Near it, there is a small lake,
At the bridge, I have a break.

I want to be light and fly,
Like a free bird in the sky.
Most of all, I like to play,
With these four friends all day!

Svitlana Rakul (8)

Paint The World Bright!

An energetic creature
Filled with electricity
Through its astonishing, cheerful
And exotic cheeks.
Its yellow, vibrant, glistening
And delightful body runs faster
And faster by the second.
After a while, it starts to generate
Electricity and builds up power,
But sadly, it's the end of
The Pikachu tour!

Evisa Dragoba (9)

Stereotypes

I'm American, which means
I must be a NJ Devils supporter,
I must be a coffee lover,
I must love PB and Js,
But I don't and am not
Anything there,
I'm British, which means
I must be a rich snob,
I must be a tea lover,
I must have terrible teeth,
But I don't and am not
Anything there.

Sonya Scott (10)

Real Love

Love is the colour of tickled pink
To write love you first need ink

A love heart is the colour red
Love opens all day until it is time for bed

Love is all about finding a crush
Also if you're lucky you might have a lush

Finally, love is about getting married
And enjoy your babies being carried.

Bradyn Pancholi (9)

Fantastic

I may not be as good as a runner as others,
Or doing maths in my head quickly, or being as good at tennis as others,
But I think this and realise...
I should focus on what I can do!
I can read well, I love playing music,
I'm quite good in goals and I love literacy
Then, I think, *this is me, this is who I am.*

Florence McDaid (9)

This Is Me

T imid, but fierce
H eartfelt, when it comes to my family
I magination floods my mind
S ushi; the one thing that's always enticing

I f you lose, you can still be a champion
S caly snakes; my enemies

M ighty, my middle name
E nergy roams within me.

Liv (11)

Horses

S o, I love riding bareback on a horse
O ver the lush green fields so far,
M y horse is as black as night with a star on his forehead moon-white.
E verybody would gasp and cheer when me and my horse came to appear.
R eally, my horse is most great and he will never tire of riding in the spotlight.

Somer Howell (8)

The Three Cs

Creative
This is me
I am creative in my walk, my talk and my smile.

Caring
I care when I greet
I care on the streets
I care whenever I can!

Considerate
I'm considerate when I learn
When I'm at home
Or with others because...

This is me!

Isabelle Djumpah-Ansah (10)

This Is Me

I weave in and out without a sound
Can you see me?
I'm over here standing tall
But still, you don't see me!
If I shouted really loud would you see me
Or would I still be invisible?
I am not a ghost, I am real and I hurt too
I am here, I am listening, and I can see
I am Lily,
This is me!

Lily McKeon (10)

Mother's Day Poem

I love my mum, she helps me every day.
She's always been with me every step of the way.
I love my mum from the bottom of my heart.
I don't know what I would do if we were apart.
I love my mum, my mum loves me,
I have the lock, she has the key.
Today is the day that I say
Happy Mother's Day!

Kaisea-Rose Brayshaw (11)

Autism Is Me

A ll of us are different
U nder all my layers
T his is who I am
I am still a person
S ome might think I'm not
M aybe I'm wrong

I am me inside
S ometimes I worry

M aybe I start to cry
E ven I am special.

Ben Allison (11)

All About Me!

H is for hilarious, always comedic
A is for awesome, a most inspiring person
M is for memorable, the days spent in my company
Z is for zesty, living life to the fullest
A is for the authenticity with which I lead life
H is for heroic, courageously stepping forth.

Hamzah Rahman (10)

A Man Wanted To Catch A Bee

A man wanted to catch a bee,
But didn't give him a fee.
He didn't pay a pound,
But he made a sound.
He was mad,
But very sad.
He heard a cricket,
But won a wicket.
He was eating beans,
But could not lean.
A man wanted to catch a bee,
But didn't give him a fee.

Akshayan Vivekanantharajah

This Is Me

This is me,
I love to read books,
And I love to write poetry,
Because poetry is me.

This is me,
I love to draw,
And paint,
It doesn't make people faint.

This is me,
A wonderful person,
Full of joy
And laughter,
So can't you see
This is me?

Syeda Anisa Mumtaz Nakvi (10)

This Is Me

The wave crash of a tsunami,
The eruption of a volcano,
A towering, snowy mountain,
This is me.

The roar of an unbeaten lion,
The beating of a hawk's wings,
A tornado in the ocean,
This is me.

The thunder rumbling at night,
The fireworks exploding in the sky,
A never-ending waterfall,
This is me!

Lauren Bennett Lazare (10)

I Am

These lines I recite before I go to bed,
These amazing lines always stay in my head,
I am bad,
I am strong,
I am fierce,
Never wrong,
I am clever,
I am bold,
I am helpful,
Never cold,
These lines I recite before I go to bed,
These amazing lines always stay in my head.

Sienna Somal (8)

This Is Me

T eachers say that I am clever
H e says that I will be forever
I think that football is the best
S ienna says otherwise...

I sla says that I am kind
S ushi is in my mind

M y art is good and bad
E quality is key all the time.

Isabella Howes-Warnes (10)

Handstand

Hard but fun they are
"Another one! Well done!"
"No way, you did it!"
"Do it again please!"
"So easy to do now!"
"Try again."
Always is a lot of fun.
"No negotiating. Do it!"
"Do a handstand, do a handstand!"

Rose Le Mer Suresh (7)

This Is Me

This is me
Sitting under a tree,
Looking up in the sky,
Thinking about how to fly,
Sliding down a rainbow,
While humming a solo,
See some pretty fairies,
Singing very merrily,
See the clouds drifting away,
Come down and say,
"What a wonderful day for (me)."

Aminah Zishan (8)

This Is Me

This is me
I love to read books
And I love to write poetry
Because poetry is me

This is me
I love to draw
And paint
It doesn't make people faint

This is me
A wonderful person
Full of joy
And laughter
So can't you see
This is me.

Syeda Anisa Mumtaz Nakvi (10)

What I Am

I am a book reader,
I am an Alex Rider fan,
I am a football lover,
I am a bulldozer in a Stopsley United shirt,
I am a video game player,
I am a cola drinker,
I am a burger muncher,
I am a crisp cruncher,
I am a bad joke maker,
I am a lie-in lover,
And most of all,
I am a good friend.
This is me.

Noah Tailor-Hooker (11)

I Am Ethan

I am Ethan and I am eight,
I think lots of animals are great,
Penguins waddle and cats meow,
Parrots speak but I don't know how,
If I was an animal I'd be a horse,
So I could run around all day, of course,
Yes, I am Ethan and I am eight,
And I think animals are great.

Ethan Jones (8)

All About Samuel

- **S** amuel is silly,
- **A** ntelopes are my favourite,
- **M** y favourite food is chicken nuggets,
- **U** mbrellas are my favourite object because they keep me dry when it's raining,
- **E** ventually, I'll become a pro at swimming,
- **L** ikes doing arts and crafts.

Samuel Kiwanuka-Musoke (7)

This Is Me!

I am a girl who is always curious,
In class, I am never serious,
My friends think I am hysterically hilarious,
I do things that are mysterious,

My brother is always furious,
But my sister is glorious,
My house is luxurious,
This is me, notorious but still curious.

Neha Shivapathy (7)

This Is Me

I like who I am
Because I am unique,
I can be the person I want to be.
I can wear my own clothes
And eat my own food
And play the music that fits my mood
I can live my own life
Or it's written for me
Who knows, we'll just have to wait and see!

Ranniel Masambique (11)

All About Me

C aring to everyone no matter what
H elps a lot. Welcomes everyone
E xcellent behaviour at school
L istens to my teacher
S ay sorry if I did something wrong
E njoys playing and making friends
A sk for help when I need it.

Princess Chelsea Ogbogu-Asogwa (10)

I Am Levi Amoah

I am Levi Amoah

- **L** oving
- **E** xtraordinary
- **V** ictorious
- **I** mportant

- **A** Christian
- **M** asterful
- **O** ne of four children
- **A** Manchester United fan
- **H** ighly intelligent.

That is me.

Levi Amoah (8)

My Goals

I am a striker,
Fanatic,
I am each of my goals.

I am defiant,
Famous,
Fascinated by fame.

I am *cccrrrackkk!*
Top of the class!
But sad when I'm sick.

I am a warrior.
A worrier.
A new way with words.

Jake Perry (9)

I Am Me

I am me,
As sweet as a bee,
Why be anyone else?
I'll just be myself,
I like to play,
It will stay that way,
Football is my favourite game,
My teacher is to blame,
I am me,
As tall as a tree,
This is my poem,
And I am very wholesome.

Delia Barnham (10)

This Is Me

I am Alexander
I strike like thunder
When I score a goal.

I dig like a mole
Until I find my ball
And then I forget it all

Sometimes I'm mean
But to hurt I don't mean
Because I am lovely
And kind to people who are mine.

Alexander Thomas Elmantawy (8)

This Is Me

S ophie is an eight-year-old girl,
O f course, she likes fossils, gems and pearls.
P refers Halloween with a scary bat,
H ow she likes to be with her cat.
I ce cream is her favourite treat,
E very day, she likes to be neat.

Sophie Pegler (8)

I Am Me

M agnificent
A ccountable
A dmirable
M odest
E nthusiastic

G enerous
Y oung
A daptable
M otivated
F riendly
U nique
A ctive
H ard-working.

Maame Gyamfuah Boateng-Bamdoh (9)

All About Me

C oming to school every day means a fresh start
O thers sometimes say I'm crazy
S aving my thoughts is tricky
M aking friends proves to be hard
A sking my mother what we are eating
S aving all my money for a new day.

Cosmas Eze (11)

Harrison

H appy is my life
A mazing is who I am
R emake things when they get destroyed
R ecreate moments
I am honest and kind
S occer is what I play
O wn up when I do something wrong
N ot afraid of things.

Harrison Pronger (8)

This Is Me

T his is me
H umorous I like to be
I maginative I guarantee
S mart most certainly

I dealistic I aim to be
S trong, you can agree

M otivated you may see
E nthusiasm is my speciality.

Markel Marinho (10)

Saviour

S uper nice and friendly
A nd lovely to all my friends
V ery much creative
I n me, you can depend.
O utside on the playground
U pstairs in our class
R emember, I will smile when I'm walking past.

Saviour Higgans (8)

What I Like

My favourite colour is rose gold
My favourite animal is a turtle
My favourite sport is football
And I don't like apples.

My favourite subject is history
I love my family
I used to like trains
And I don't like vegetables.

Oscar Cormack (8)

The Pains

I love to game,
In the gym, I love to gain.
The bullying has always been a pain,
I feel like I am never the main,
They laugh in shame.

I have always loved my family,
Even when I have been hurting,
Because they make me happy.

Jack Sadler (11)

Why Me?

Why me?
Why did you choose me?
All the people in the world
And it was me
Why?
Left my heart broken
Crying on the bathroom floor
Feeling angry and disappointed
But why me?
Screaming loud
Why me?
Tears rolling.

Amy Smiley (15)

This Is Me

I am brave.
I am kind.
I never give up.
I like cats.
I am helpful.
I like nature.
I am a kind friend.
I like fruit and vegetables.
I am unique.
I like the park.
I like dogs.
I love my family.
I am me!

Sophia Junglas (8)

I Am... Me

Sometimes I can be the Wizard of Oz,
Or Puss in Boots,
Or Demon Slayer,
Or a ninja.
It depends on the curtain that is left,
Sometimes my avatar answers on my behalf.
Only when my mother calls me,
Finally, I am... *Me!*

Andreea Maria Alexe (8)

All About Me

I like flowers
I enjoy going in the garden
And picking them for hours.
I love all the colours of the rainbow
Red, orange, yellow, green, blue, indigo
And violet.
When I grow up I want to be
A part-time poet, not a pilot.

Olivia Chidwick (11)

Harry

H arry is my name and I love it
A llergies I have and they make me unwell
R aces I like, but I always lose
R ides that are scary and fast make me happy
Y ou can call me Haribo because that is my nickname.

Harry Warren (9)

Refuge

An oasis of calm far away from everything
The place where I can really be me
Absent from fear, loneliness and doubt
A sanctuary which is safe, peaceful, calm and tranquil
When the darkness has taken hold
There I find true light.

Thomas Potter (11)

This Is Me

A kennings poem

I am a...
Friend finder
Polite asker
Sandwich eater
Fizzy drinker
Spider speeder
Funny joker
Sports watcher
Good helper
Shy speaker
Game player
Deep sleeper
And finally...
A fab worker!

William Hogley (11)

My Life

D WA is my dance group,
A street dance team, which
N ever gives up
C hloe is our leader and guide
E ntertainment, fitness, friendship and fun are our goals
R emaining together forever!

Sophie Goodier (11)

Friendship

Beauty, neatness, calm.
Clearness, feelings left unharmed.
None of which I possess,
yet people remain charmed.
How come I feel this way? That I do not know.
But to all of you out there,
You can never go too slow.

Nancy Rossiter-Pointer (10)

Conrad

I am funny and I am kind
I love reading, if you don't mind
Books take you away to wonderful places
Where you go to new worlds and meet new faces
Adventure stories are really great
I love reading and I am eight.

Conrad Jones (8)

This Is Me!

I am the king
I love to sing

Sport is my life
Cricket is no strife
In rugby on the wing
I drive and cling
I love to thrash
I love to bash
In cricket, I like to smash
I will mash!

I'm such an amazing thing!

Charlie Thomas (8)

School Adventure

S chool is the best,
C an do learning all day,
H ome is six hours away,
O pening books, expanding our minds,
O ur school also loves fun,
L et's take a knowledge ride!

Zuriel Oyedeji (8)

All About Me!

B rave
L ucky
A mazing
K ind
E xcellent writer

L ively
A wesome
G reat
O ptimistic
D aring
A ctive.

Blake Lagoda (10)

All About Me

My name is Xander, my parents call me Boo Bell,
My hobbies are Lego; collecting toy cars as well.
My parents say I'm funny, I guess I could agree,
That's the end of this poem, thanks for listening to me.

Xander Blyth Bell (9)

This Is Me

A n amazing personality
M agnificently good at maths
E nthusiastic about everything
L ove my cat
I ndependent at everything
A stonishing at acting.

Amelia Reilly (10)

Victor

V ictor is my name
I am the same
C ategory in every subject
T hat can make you eject
O r lose your concentration
R unning from the sensation.

Victor Umahi Ndiwe (11)

This Is Me

S ienna is very smiley
I like foxes
E verybody should look after the environment
N ever drops litter
N ature is beautiful
A lways be kind.

Sienna Jefferson (8)

This Is Me

Brother number three
Blonde buddy
Lego fan
Chess trickster
Sloth lover
Book maniac
Minecraft master
Friend of flowers
Blue-eyed boy

...That is me!

Archie Pugh (7)

Tanya Huhn

T all
A mbitious
N ice
Y outhful
A ccomplished

H eaven's angel
U nique
H onourable
N oble.

Tanya Huhn (11)

The Marvellous Me!
A diamante poem

Me
Sporty, curious
Climbing, laughing, fishing
Loves collecting Pokémon cards, agile, quick passes
Throwing, catching, shooting
Adventurous, kind
Footballer.

Harry Chalk (9)

Chloe To Bilbo

My name is Chloe
But my family call me Bilbo
Because I am:

- **B** rilliant
- **I** ntelligent
- **L** earning
- **B** rave
- **O** riginal.

Chloe Rose (8)

A Limerick

You can never get me,
I'm a little hard-working bee,
By raising the bar,
I'll shine like a star,
This is super-duper me!

Muhammed Luqman Arafath (7)

Me And My World

A diamante poem

Me
Messy, smart
Sparkling, loving, sharing
Happy to help, loves to play
Caring, creating, drawing
Silly, brave
Girl.

Elizabeth Dymond (9)

How To Make Great Sentences

How to make great sentences...

Capital letters and full stops
Handwriting
Adjectives
Punctuation
Spellings.

Charlotte Bundred (10)

Julia

J umps every day
U ses common sense
L oves to sleep
I maginative
A mazing at sport.

Julia Falecka (11)

Summertime

It's summertime
Let's make a rhyme
The grass is green so feel free
Today's your day so say hooray!

Safa Khalil

Rabia

R emarkable
A rtistic
B rave
I rritating
A ggressive.

Rabia Dar (11)

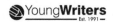

Soman Chainani

- **S** pectacular
- **O** bliging
- **M** acho
- **A** mazing
- **N** arrator.

Rose Blundell (10)

YOUNG WRITERS INFORMATION

We hope you have enjoyed reading this book – and that you will continue to in the coming years.

If you're the parent or family member of an enthusiastic poet or story writer, do visit our website **www.youngwriters.co.uk/subscribe** and sign up to receive news, competitions, writing challenges and tips, activities and much, much more! There's lots to keep budding writers motivated!

If you would like to order further copies of this book, or any of our other titles, then please give us a call or order via your online account.

Young Writers
Remus House
Coltsfoot Drive
Peterborough
PE2 9BF
(01733) 890066
info@youngwriters.co.uk

Join in the conversation!
Tips, news, giveaways and much more!

YoungWritersUK   **YoungWritersCW**   **youngwriterscw**

Scan me to watch the This Is Me video!